Scholastic WORKSHOP

KEY STAGE 1 / SCOTTISH LEVELS A-B

NON-FICTION
Writing Skills

SALLIE HARKNESS,
LYNDA KEITH &
JOYCE LINDSAY

Published by Scholastic Ltd,
Villiers House,
Clarendon Avenue,
Leamington Spa,
Warwickshire CV32 5PR
Text © 1997 Sallie Harkness, Lynda Keith and Joyce Lindsay
© 1997 Scholastic Ltd
3 4 5 6 7 8 9 0   9 0 1 2 3 4 5 6

Authors
Sallie Harkness, Lynda Keith and Joyce Lindsay

Project Consultants
Sue Ellis and Gill Friel

Editor
Joel Lane

Assistant Editor
Kate Pearce

Series Designer
Joy White

Designer
Louise Belcher

Illustrations
Kim Woolley

Cover illustration
Joy White

Designed using Aldus Pagemaker

British Library Cataloguing-in-Publication Date
A catalogue record for this book
is available from the British Library.

ISBN 0-590-53478-5

Contents

5 Chapter One

INTRODUCTION

15 Chapter Two

ASSESSMENT

25 Chapter Three

INFORMATION WRITING

73 Chapter Four

PERSUASION AND DISCUSSION

123 Chapter Five

INSTRUCTIONS AND DIRECTIONS

ACKNOWLEDGEMENTS

The publishers gratefully acknowledge permission to reproduce the following copyright material:

Hodder Headline plc for the illustration and text extract from *Save This Tree* by Maggie Pearson and Jacqui Thomas © 1991, Maggie Pearson and Jacqui Thomas (1991, Hodder and Stoughton).

Suzi Jenkin-Pearce for the illustration and **Caroline Sheldon Literary Agent** for Kate Umansky's permission to use a redrawn and adapted illustration from *Tiger and Me* by Kate Umansky © 1990, illustration Suzi Jenkin-Pearce (1990, Red Fox).

Calum Lindsay for the text of 'Calum's letter' and the accompanying illustration © 1997, Calum Lindsay.

Reed Consumer Books Ltd for text and an adaptation from *The Owl Who Was Afraid of the Dark* by Jill Tomlinson © 1992, Jill Tomlinson (1992, Mammoth Books).

Walker Books Ltd for illustrations and text from *How To Look After Your Cat* by Colin and Jacqui Hawkins © 1982 Colin and Jacqui Hawkins (1982, 1996 Walker Books Ltd) and extracts and illustrations from *The Fantastic Football Fun Book* by Alan Durant © text 1994, Alan Durant © illustrations 1994, Cathy Gale (1994, Walker Books Ltd).

Scholastic
WORKSHOP

Chapter One
INTRODUCTION

NON-FICTION WRITING SKILLS

Young children are eager to write. They witness adults writing and responding to written forms as part of their daily lives. They know that writing is an important and powerful form of communication in the adult world.

This resource is designed to help teachers:
• build on children's motivation and encourage their positive attitudes;
• tune into and develop the children's knowledge and understanding of non-fiction writing;
• help children to develop the understanding needed to write for a variety of purposes and audiences.

The book helps teachers to focus on key teaching and learning issues in an interesting, balanced and effective way, within contexts which are meaningful to young children.

Teaching non-fiction writing

Traditionally, non-fiction writing in the early stages of primary education has been taught in two ways: either through one-off activities within the context of a class project (such as designing a poster about cleaning your teeth) or through a skills lesson emphasising a particular structure (for instance, how to write a letter). Much of the teaching input was focused on the layout and format of the piece of writing produced. Teachers often taught children how to write 'a poster' or 'a letter', focusing on the format alone. That a

poster, for example, might serve different functions such as to inform, persuade or instruct, each of which involves different organisational and language features, was frequently given scant recognition.

Genres of non-fiction writing

Genre theory provides a new and different focus for the teaching of non-fiction writing. The primary emphasis is on the **purpose** of a piece of writing, rather than its format. Thus, for example, a letter may recount experiences, give instructions or try to persuade. To become effective writers, young children need to recognise the different purposes of non-fiction writing and – through discussion and explicit teaching – begin to learn the organisational features and language characteristics that each purpose requires.

Much of the work on genre theory has come from analysis of adult writing and of writing in the secondary school curriculum. Genres can be complex: people create new genres by writing for new and different purposes. Classifying writing – especially young children's writing – according to genre can be difficult and should not be seen as an end in itself. However, there are two reasons why it can be useful and relevant, in the early stages of primary education, to recognise the key genres which are most appropriate to the experiences of primary-age children:
• Firstly, the genres provide a framework which allows the teacher quickly to identify appropriate vocabulary and organisational features which might form the teaching content for any piece of writing.

• Secondly, the different genres involve organising and presenting knowledge in different ways. Teachers need to be familiar with the range of genres and to appreciate how they can serve different learning objectives. This knowledge and understanding will enable them to select and structure appropriate writing tasks to deepen children's learning.

Key genres in the primary school

The key genres of non-fiction reading and writing on which the Scholastic Non-Fiction Writing Workshops are based are the following.

Recount writing: to recount a sequence of events, usually told in the order in which they occurred. This is possibly the closest form of non-fiction writing to a story. When children write about what happened on a school trip, how a tadpole develops into a frog or how they conducted an experiment in science, they often write in this genre.

Report writing: to provide factual information about a topic. This is the genre adopted in many non-fiction books. The writer identifies a number of key issues and writes clearly and concisely about each. Writing about topics for class and individual projects often takes this form. Unless the activity is carefully structured, many primary-age children may end up copying chunks of text from books when asked to write in this genre.

Explanatory writing: to explain how and why something happens or works. This type of writing is often combined with report or recount writing. Children are often required to write explanations of such phenomena as how a model works, what causes a boat to float, how

puddles are formed or why Wellington boots keep out the rain.

Procedural writing: to instruct others in carrying out a process. Children do this when they write directions to tell others how to get to their house, a recipe for a favourite meal, instructions for making a model or using a particular piece of equipment, or (sometimes) the rules for a game.

Persuasive writing: to persuade others to adopt a particular (often the persuader's own) point of view. Children do this when they write advertising posters and slogans, or speeches to present a particular argument in a debate.

Discussion writing: to state a particular issue or question, compare different viewpoints and reach a reasoned conclusion. Children do this when they examine conflicting views on an issue such as care of the environment, or look at the reasons why different people have different tastes or beliefs.

For the purpose of this book, we have grouped these genres under three main headings:

• **Instructions and directions:** This is essentially procedural writing, including orders and rules as well as instructions on how to make something, recipes and directions for how to get somewhere.

• **Persuasion and discussion:** This is writing to persuade others, or to present different viewpoints and reach a conclusion (though the latter often poses problems for young writers).

• **Information writing:** This includes recounts, reports and explanations, which have certain features in common.

These three categories are explored in more detail in the chapters which follow.

NATIONAL CURRICULUM GUIDELINES

In planning work in all areas of the curriculum teachers will refer to the National Curriculum for England and Wales or the Scottish 5–14 Guidelines.

The National Curriculum for England and Wales requires that children will begin to:
• *draw messages through pictures* (Key Stage 1 Level 1);
• *be aware of written communication around the classroom* (KS1 Level 2);
• *recognise different purposes for writing, e.g. messages, letters, labels, stories and explanations* (KS1 Level 2);
• *relinquish dominant personal narratives and offer some third-person narrative* (KS1 Level 2);
• *show increasing confidence to talk about non-fiction topics and be willing to discuss how this could best be presented in written form, e.g. through plans, diagrams and descriptions* (KS1 Level 3);
• *negotiate many written ways of expressing and presenting ideas* (KS1 Level 3).

The Scottish 5–14 Guidelines set the purposes of functional writing as being: *to convey information; to order, clarify, record and reflect on ideas, experiences and opinions.*

Children are asked to:
• *write for a simple practical purpose* (Level A);
• *write briefly in an appropriate form for a variety of practical purposes* (Level B).

The Scottish 5–14 Programmes of Study make it clear that such writing will arise in the context of other classroom activities *such as planting seeds, giving directions, exploring technology, baking and so on. Pupils will discuss before, during and after the activity. They will report orally to teacher and others.* They suggest that *sequence can be explored through drawings, perhaps linked by arrows, to form a flow chart. The teacher will help pupils to observe, to select important features, to order their writing and act as a scribe* (Level A)

At Level B, *appropriate forms might include letters or reports about events or activities undertaken. Sequencing will continue. Pupils may perhaps use simple notes to order their writing. Audiences for letters can include other pupils, parents, people in the community. Motivation is best given by writing real letters – to an author, to a newspaper, seeking information and so on. Teachers will make pupils aware of writing styles and the vocabulary suitable for different audiences, and demonstrate layout features.*

WHY LEARN NON-FICTION WRITING?

Children are surrounded by texts in school, in the street or the supermarket, at home and on television. They see adults writing shopping lists, noting phone numbers, filling in forms, marking registers. Children are motivated to join this literate world as writers, and it is important that adults encourage and help them. In writing non-fiction, children need to communicate for functional purposes, and must learn to write clearly and concisely for different purposes and readers.

Writing non-fiction also helps children to organise their thoughts and communicate them clearly to others. It is a major tool for learning across the curriculum. Discussing, framing, re-framing, selecting, presenting and explaining their ideas helps children to remember and to understand. These skills will be essential as children move up the primary school and into the more formal assessment systems of secondary education, where the ability to write clearly, concisely and for specific purposes is essential within all areas of the curriculum. The knowledge and understanding they will need starts in these early stages.

What children need to learn about non-fiction writing

Recent work on child development (such as that of Gordon Wells in language and Martin Hughes in mathematics) recognises children as 'active constructors' of their own learning. This view places emphasis on what children already know and can do; on children as thinkers, asking questions and enquiring to find answers; on children making connections and accommodating new knowledge into what they already know, developing a deeper understanding. Children's intellectual capacity should not be underestimated.

Traditionally, the area of writing has not involved enquiry and exploration. Writing has been viewed purely as a skill to be taught. Sometimes this has resulted in an emphasis on handwriting and form rather than on content and purpose. The updated view of the child as an active learner gives teachers the opportunity to look at children and writing in a new light. The starting point for teaching is what the children already know and can do. As indicated above, this may amount to a great deal in terms of the purposes and formats of functional writing.

In the early stages, children need to explore and experiment with sending messages in 'writing'. Early attempts may be made in scribble writing, which may develop into 'pseudo-writing' and later into something which is more recognisable to adults as intelligible writing. Young children need to build up confidence as writers and not be overly concerned with correctness. They need to be encouraged to take risks and try out their ideas. While children must be aware that writing (functional or otherwise) is about communication, and that clear handwriting, accurate spelling and correct punctuation can all aid effective communication, these aspects must be taught and discussed in a way that does not engender a fear of being criticised for wrong spelling, wrong punctuation or badly-formed letters. Teachers across the UK might debate the relative importance of these elements at different stages of the primary school. However, what really matters is:

• what teachers know about what children can do and the children's knowledge and experience;

• how teachers provide opportunities and contexts which lead naturally to children's functional writing;

• how teachers respond to children's attempts to send messages in writing;

• how teachers focus on children's varying needs and abilities, and target their teaching in a differentiated way.

Teachers need to help children achieve the learning objectives given in the National Curriculum and Scottish 5–14 Guidelines. They also need to recognise that these learning objectives can be achieved in a variety of different ways.

TEACHING, LEARNING AND USING THIS BOOK

This book and its companion volume, *Non-Fiction Writing Projects*, contextualise children's learning about functional writing and its genres in situations which will be familiar to children from real life. Children can recognise a great variety of types of, and purposes for, functional

writing in their environment. The adult's response to the child's perceptions of environmental print is significant in developing the child's literacy skills. Adults must notice children's interest, knowledge and understanding, and praise their attempts.

Using real examples from children's lives can stimulate their interest. These examples can be used to teach the key elements of the different genres. A menu from the local pizza restaurant, a railway ticket, an advertising leaflet from the local shop – any of these can be investigated to focus on key features of structure and layout, language, visual impact, audience and purpose. The children can use real examples as models to create their own.

A useful resource for the teacher to build up would be a 'Genre Box' containing a collection of leaflets, posters, tickets, recipes, menus, instructions, directions, maps and plans. Children will enjoy adding to this, and it will be a valuable resource for work on functional reading and writing. The link between reading for information and functional writing is clearly made in the activities throughout this book.

The activities provided do not always have a written outcome, as this may be inappropriate for the stage of the children or the particular task. Children will be involved in selecting, sorting, matching, ordering and labelling, as well as in creating formats and written text.

How to teach non-fiction writing

Every teacher has her/his own teaching style and her/his own beliefs about teaching and learning. These will influence the writing curriculum as much as any other curriculum. Across the UK, a range of teaching and learning

Information box

modes will be in evidence. At one extreme, children will be encouraged to practise free exploration in mark-making and writing. These children will see themselves as creating 'writing', but may have little adult guidance and support. At the other extreme, children may be discouraged from writing until they have mastered the technical skill of letter formation. These children may use pictures to send messages, with adults scribing for them. They may view themselves as being unable to write and create messages. Many teachers will find themselves working somewhere between these two extremes.

This book emphasises the importance of a learner-centred curriculum: a curriculum which recognises where children are and what they know and can do, but also where they will need help and support to develop their skills in, and their knowledge and understanding of, functional writing. It also recognises the wide variety of ways in which this help and support can be offered by the teacher. The activities suggested are adaptable to a wide variety of settings, and to a wide variety of teaching and learning modes.

Balancing context and content, process and product

Functional writing needs to be taught in the classroom. But should it be taught within the writing curriculum, focusing on a particular skill or the understanding of a particular genre, or should it be integrated into what may be a more natural and meaningful context for the children? Giving instructions on how to look after a pet is a writing (or a reading, selecting and ordering) task, but it will have more meaning within an environmental topic than set purely as a writing exercise. However, one difficulty which arises with the latter approach is that children face not only the demands of the writing task, but also those of the content or subject. This challenge is met here by providing both activities planned within a wider context and activities intended as separate, almost 'one-off', experiences aimed at developing specific knowledge and understanding and/or skills.

Play and planning

Play provides a natural medium for the integration of functional writing. The appointments book and posters in the hairdressing salon or the menu and waiter's notebook in the class restaurant provide ideal opportunities for the teacher to plan functional writing, giving the children created but 'real' purposes and audiences. The teacher may choose to follow up free play opportunities with more formal teaching, or may do the formal teaching before allowing the children to practise the taught skills in a play session. The direct teaching needs a light touch, and should be centred on children's current concerns and understandings. Teachers can tune into these through observation of children in different situations and through discussion of their writing – its purposes and readership, its clarity and cohesion, its structure, genre and format, and its language. This will be done individually and in group or class settings. Children's awareness of all these aspects must be raised and discussed in order to develop their writing skills and their knowledge and understanding of writing.

Even very young children can handle these difficult ideas in the right context. For example, a group of seven-year-olds might decide to make a joke book to sell on Red Nose Day. They decide to advertise in the class for jokes, and develop a system for collecting jokes. A poster seems the best method for this. They naturally will need to make the poster eye-catching, and to make sure that it includes all the necessary information in a clear, concise form. The teacher could help to make these points explicit in their discussions.

This discussion of writing – the process as well as the end product – gives both the teacher and the child useful information on what is known and understood, and where to go next. This will allow the teacher to consider the best route forward for the child, and the most appropriate way to scaffold the child's learning.

USING THIS RESOURCE

Teachers can use this book to plan in a coherent way, in order to ensure progression in the development of children's skills in, and knowledge and understanding of, the different genres of functional writing.

Components of the Writing Workshop

This *Scholastic Writing Workshop* is made up of two complementary books. *Non-Fiction Writing Skills* provides focused, single-lesson activities that highlight and explore key aspects of specific genres. The book provides:
• ideas for short, focused activities that target the five main genres (grouped into three chapters for continuity between related genres);
• photocopiable activity and resource sheets to support teaching and learning;
• suggestions, advice and photocopiable pages for assessment and record keeping.

Non-Fiction Writing Projects details extended writing projects that integrate a variety of genres within single projects, encouraging children to write for real purposes and real readers. This generates high motivation and emotional involvement, making evaluation a truly meaningful process. The book provides:
• ideas and lesson plans for whole-class or group projects;
• photocopiable activity sheets;
• ideas for publishing, celebrating and evaluating the children's work;
• suggestions, advice and photocopiable pages for assessment and record-keeping.

The tightly-framed lessons in this volume can help teachers to explore a specific genre in depth or to plan coverage of a range of genres. The extended contexts from the *Non-Fiction Writing Projects* book support and target different genres, but also provide real contexts with real readers. Children's high level of emotional and social engagement will lead to an equally high commitment to making their writing effective.

Some teachers may choose to plan the work of the class around a succession of non-fiction writing projects, including genre-focused activities as and when they are necessary to ensure a balanced coverage, or in response to things they have noticed about the children's writing. Other teachers may plan to cover a series of specific genres through the focused activities in this volume and then choose a complementary non-fiction writing project to do as a sort of creative break with the class.

Where to start

A topic-only approach may lead to a lack of continuity and coherence, and consequently to a disjointed progression. Teachers need to understand the skills they are teaching and to plan for progressive and coherent development.

One important role for the teacher is in modelling the writing process. Following the example of a more experienced writer can help children to recognise the need for planning their writing, for reviewing what they write, or for rehearsing, drafting, revising and editing. Whatever the preferred terminology, the teacher's role is to help pupils first to look, think and talk (about purpose, audience, content, structure and so on), then to write and draw, and finally to reflect and discuss. This may lead to some redrafting; but in the early years, this may be inappropriate. It is important to remember that at this stage – Reception to Year 2 (Scottish P1 to P3) – process may be more important than product.

The successful use of the activities in this book depends on a positive and open relationship between teacher and pupils – one in which the children see themselves as writers, albeit emergent. The teacher should select and, if necessary, adapt activities to suit the needs and experience of the children. A regular review by the teacher of each child's progress is essential; this allows the selection of appropriate tasks and activities to support further development and strengthen skills. Tasks or activities may be undertaken by children working individually, in pairs or in small groups, or by the whole class working together. There are clear advantages in having the children work with a partner or in a small group, creating a real purpose and an audience.

Activities of this kind will be found most relevant by the children in a classroom where active learning is encouraged through structured play experience, including the following: use of sand and water; construction using kits and junk materials; table-top games and activities; a range of art and craft materials and activities; involvement in imaginative role play; investigation of the natural world (for example, by growing plants); and access to a well-stocked library, including a range of information books as well as fiction titles.

Talk is an important means of developing ideas. Planned time for talk before, during and after the writing activities is essential.

Children should have opportunities to experience working in different groupings. In these activities, the children are sometimes grouped according to ability and sometimes working in mixed-ability groups. Sometimes they will work with the teacher and at other times work independently. Group size will also vary, from pairs and threes to large groups. The material is designed for a classroom which has been organised to give the children some independence.

Layout and organisation of this book

The tasks and activities vary in their level of difficulty, and in the demands they make on children's ability to collaborate. The chart provided on page 14 classifies the activities according to their main focus, thus making coherent planning simpler. Ideas and formats for record-keeping and assessment are also included. (See Chapter Two.)

The structure of each lesson plan is as follows (also see the Key to Symbols Used box opposite):
• **Level of difficulty** is indicated by a star rating. Activities with one star are the easiest in terms of content level and amount of support given. Three-star activities are the most difficult and are aimed at older or more experienced children. Where the content or type of activity is new, one-star activities provide a good starting point for all children. Some activities may be adapted to suit the age or ability of the children across this range, and are thus given the star rating ✱|✱|✱|✱|✱.
• **Time** needed for the activity is indicated by a clock symbol. More than one session may be

indicated. A blank clock symbol indicates an unfixed amount of time, which may extend over several sessions.
• **Class organisation** indicates whether the activity involves children working individually, in pairs, in a small group or as a class.
• **Teaching content** explains the main teaching point of the activity.
• **What you need** lists the resources required for the session, including any photocopiable pages needed to support the activity.
• **What to do** describes each activity, explaining how to make the teaching points and raise particular issues for discussion.
• **Further development** gives ideas for developing the activity further, or for applying it to different contexts.

Bibliography

Browne, Ann *Helping Children To Write*, Paul Chapman Publishing Ltd, 1993.
Calkins, Lucy M. *The Art of Teaching Writing*, Irwin Publishing, 1994.
Clay, Marie M. *Writing Begins at Home*, Heinemann, 1992.
Hall, Nigel (ed.) *Writing With Reason*, Hodder & Stoughton, 1992.
Lewis, Maureen and Wray, David *Developing Children's Non-Fiction Writing: working with writing frames*, Scholastic, 1995.
Whitehead, M.R. *Language and Literacy in the Early Years*, Paul Chapman Publishing Ltd, 1990.

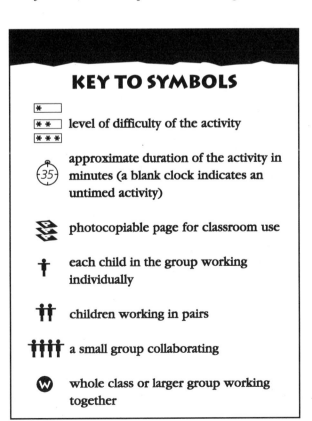

KEY TO SYMBOLS

✱ / ✱✱ / ✱✱✱ level of difficulty of the activity

(35) approximate duration of the activity in minutes (a blank clock indicates an untimed activity)

photocopiable page for classroom use

† each child in the group working individually

†† children working in pairs

†††† a small group collaborating

Ⓦ whole class or larger group working together

TEACHING CONTENT	Recognising audience and purpose	Selecting and organising ideas	Selecting formats	Sequencing	Using persuasive language	Giving appropriate reasonse	Using words to indicate action, sequence or direction	Using pictures and diagrams
INFORMATION WRITING	5, 6, 8, 20	1, 4, 9, 11, 14, 15, 17	2, 13, 18	7, 19		12		3, 10, 16
PERSUASION AND DISCUSSION	All activities	9, 10	11, 12, 13		1, 3, 5, 7, 8, 17	2, 4, 6, 14, 15		16, 18, 19
INSTRUCTIONS AND DIRECTIONS	1, 2, 3, 4	7	9	5, 6, 8, 10	12		11, 13, 14	15, 16, 17, 18, 19, 20, 21

Note: These numbers refer to activity numbers.

Scholastic WORKSHOP

Chapter Two,

ASSESSMENT

ASSESSMENT

Assessment in *Non-Fiction Writing Skills (Key Stage 1)* is used to:
• help teachers to focus on the key features of each genre;
• use these to provide criteria for assessing children's non-fiction writing;
• provide information for planning, based on children's needs and interests;
• help children to explore their attitudes towards and feelings about non-fiction writing;
• help children to become aware of what they know, and enable the teacher to build upon this to provide progression.

Assessment should be based equally upon the process in which the child is involved and the 'end product' of non-fiction writing. The teacher needs to know:
• *How confident are the children about starting the writing task?*
• *Do they realise that someone will read their work?*
• *What has to be written?*
• *How will it be written?*
• *Who will read it?*
• *Can they talk about what was easy/difficult in the writing activity?*

A key strategy for assessment is discussion with the children and observation of them during the task, both in play situations and in evaluating their work. By engaging children in discussion and reflection, the teacher will gain more evidence of their level of awareness.

General assessment and record-keeping photocopiables (pages 19–24)

Six photocopiable sheets for assessment and record-keeping are provided in this book. They can be used alongside the activities to build up a cumulative profile of individual and group achievement.

Individual/group notes (pages 19–21)

The format of these three photocopiable sheets reflects the key areas for assessment identified in the introductions to the chapters on Persuasion and Discussion, Instructions and Directions and Information Writing.

Notes can be made under each of the headings on the sheet to:
• provide evidence of children's knowledge and understanding;
• identify particular strengths and areas for further learning.

Each sheet should record the progression of an individual or a group.

The overview grid at the beginning of each of these three chapters will also identify specific teaching and learning points which can be assessed through the individual activities in the chapter.

Some of the following questions may help to form criteria for assessing work in the genre of **persuasion and discussion**, and identifying appropriate evidence to record:

Recognises purpose and audience
Can the child recognise:
- why he/she is giving instructions?
- who he/she is giving them to?

Can sequence and structure
Can the child:
- use relevant logical steps?
- write clear, easy-to-follow steps which can be tested?
- use a structure such as: title, what you need, what you do?

Uses appropriate words to indicate action, sequence, direction
- How does the child use the words *first, then, next, finally, behind, in front, forward, back, mix, put, move*?
- Does the child use the present tense?

Uses pictures and diagrams appropriately
- Is the child aware that pictures and diagrams give messages?
- Can the child recognise the significant features of a recipe or a poster?

Similar questions can be generated to assess **information writing**.

Evidence in the form of examples will provide the most effective information to record for assessment. Thus a teacher might record: *Martin – instructions written for feeding a dog, concise with title, what you need and method. Added diagram to show the steps. Said the instructions were for his aunt. Suggested he give this writing to her and ask her if it works.*

Recognises purpose and audience
- Who is the child writing to persuade? Why is s/he writing?
- What is the best way to persuade the audience?
- What is the discussion about? What are the viewpoints? Who is involved?

Offers a point of view
- Can the child convince others?
- Can he/she state a case? Can he/she pose arguments?
- Can he/she recognise different points of view? Can he/she reach a conclusion and summarise?

Gives appropriate reasons
- How does the child justify her/his choice?

Uses persuasive language
- Can the child use words and phrases such as *because, therefore, so, I think..., I believe...?* How does she/he use these expressions?

From the above, it is clear that progression will depend largely on the child's previous experience and access to new experiences in which the skills of persuading and discussing can be developed through play and planned activities, set within contexts which are meaningful to them and enable them to practise, consolidate and extend their writing skills.

Similar questions may be devised for assessing work on **instructions and directions**:

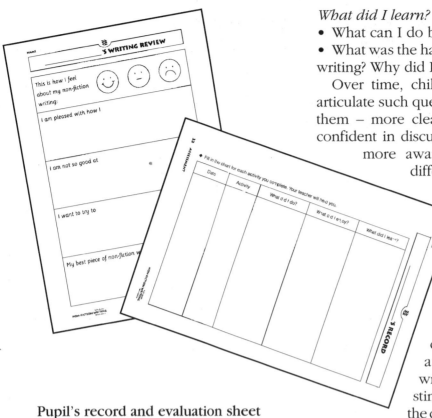

What did I learn?

- What can I do better now than before?
- What was the hardest thing about doing this writing? Why did I find that hard?

Over time, children will become able to articulate such questions – and the answers to them – more clearly as they become more confident in discussion with the teacher and more aware of the features of the different genres. This record sheet could effectively be used in conjunction with the pupil writing review sheet.

Pupil writing review (page 23)

This sheet has been designed to encourage children to look reflectively at their own non-fiction writing. It provides an effective stimulus to discussion between the child and the teacher to assess the child's writing development over a period of time. It can be used effectively for reviewing several pieces of work within a profile, and will help the teacher and the child to identify strengths and areas for future learning. It may also provide a focus for discussion of the differences between imaginative and non-fiction writing.

This sheet can be used to review work in different genres. It helps to provide evidence of the children's attitude towards writing, and may be useful in discussing their progress with parents or other teachers.

Pupil's record and evaluation sheet (page 22)

This record has been designed to be completed by an individual child in discussion with the teacher. Scribing may be necessary. It provides a record of the activities undertaken, and helps the child to consider:

What did I do?

- What was the activity about?
- What did I contribute?
- What did I make?

What did I enjoy?

- Was I interested in this? Did I want to do it?
- How easy or difficult was it?

Class (or group) record of activities (page 24)

This record sheet lists all of the activities in Chapters 3 to 5. It can be used to follow a class or group through the school, serving as a record of the activities covered in each year. It can also be used to identify the relative numbers of activities covered in different genres.

GIVING INFORMATION

Key features

Recognises purpose and audience

Selects, organises and sequences relevant information

Uses appropriate language

Selects and employs appropriate formats

PERSUASION/DISCUSSION

Key features

Recognises purpose and audience
Offers a point of view
Gives appropriate reasons
Uses persuasive language

INSTRUCTIONS/DIRECTIONS

Key features

Recognises purpose and audience

Can sequence and structure

Uses appropriate words to indicate action, sequence, direction

Uses pictures and diagrams appropriately

NAME

_____'S RECORD

◆ Fill in the chart for each activity you complete. Your teacher will help you.

Date	Activity	What did I do?	What did I enjoy?	What did I learn?

Scholastic
NON-FICTION WRITING
Workshop

_____'S WRITING REVIEW

This is how I feel about my non-fiction writing:

I am pleased with how I

I am not so good at

I want to try to

My best piece of non-fiction writing is

CLASS RECORD OF ACTIVITIES

Activities	R/P1	Y1/P2	Y2/P3	Activities	R/P1	Y1/P2	Y2/P3
Giving information				11. Toenails			
1. The weather today				12. TV advert			
2. Hobbies Factfile				13. Free gift			
3. Cool clothes				14. Where should we go?			
4. Find the facts				15. Good pet/bad pet			
5. A letter from Calum				16. Special offer			
6. Something precious				17. Bring and buy sale			
7. What I did at school today				18. Say you'll be there			
8. Baby Bear has his say				19. Oat Crispies or Rice Flakes			
9. Read the label							
10. My favourite sandwich				*Instructions and directions*			
11. What is a glossary?				1. Rules for the sand area			
12. Can you explain why?				2. How to play dominoes			
13. What's in the leaflet?				3. How to make a birthday card			
14. Designing a leaflet				4. Find the treasure			
15. All about us				5. Mixed-up instructions			
16. How I made this model				6. How to order a pizza by phone			
17. Classroom Newsdesk				7. Lost in a forest			
18. We need a class noticeboard				8. How to make a LEGO tower			
19. Classroom calendar				9. Recipe for boy soup			
20. Happy Something To You				10. How to operate a video recorder			
				11. Telling words			
Persuasion and discussion				12. How to choose			
1. Bedtime in summer				13. Our own rules			
2. Boxed in!				14. The big breakfast			
3. Save this tree				15. My route to school			
4. Dark is good				16. Say it with pictures			
5. Keep tigers in the jungle				17. Warning signs			
6. Would you rather...?				18. Paint mixing			
7. Help Little Red Riding Hood				19. Don't do that			
8. Read this book				20. At the airport			
9. The missing pieces				21. Recipe for a sandwich			
10. Big? Bad? Who, me?							

Scholastic
WORKSHOP

Chapter Three

INFORMATION WRITING

INTRODUCTION

Information (referential) writing includes recounts, reports and explanations which give information about:
1. What happened to me (**recount**) – for example, personal letters; diaries; accounts of visits, events and experiences.
2. How things are (**report**) – for example, the outcome of an experiment; the results of a survey; a weather report; a factfile on football or food.
3. Why things happen (**explanation**) – for example, how a tadpole becomes a frog, how a telephone works, why rain falls. Children at Key Stage 1/Levels A and B will 'explain' in their own way, at their own level. Their ability to progress from a description to a full explanation (in terms of causes and effects) will develop with time.

Why is information writing so important?

This is the kind of writing most frequently used in adult life. Children are likely to have seen family members using information writing to get things done at home (for example, writing a shopping list) and teachers using it when writing reports. Information writing helps in carrying out tasks, and creates permanent written records of events and decisions. It is essential in the world of business and in education, and gives power to those who use it. In everyday life, people commonly read for information (for instance, sports results).

Information writing functions as a means of organising and clarifying ideas. The ability to handle information, and particularly to express

it in writing, helps to further children's understanding of an increasingly complex world. At school, children are expected to use information writing in many areas of the curriculum. They will be expected to compile lists, to write personal accounts of events, to make notes and create information sheets, and to write reports of science experiments.

Information writing is thus a useful and relevant skill which children should practise from the earliest stages of their development as writers.

What information do children already have?

Children entering primary school have knowledge of a variety of subjects; but the information is likely to be highly contextualised and personal because each child's experience and interests are unique. Thus the teacher's problem is not so much that children lack information as that the information they have may be difficult to access. Two general strategies can be used:
1. Find ways of accessing the information and interests that children already have by talking to them and their parents, observing their play, and examining and discussing their drawings, paintings and constructions.
2. Ensure that they develop new interests and extend their knowledge by offering a range of stimulating 'in-school' experiences which can be shared and discussed.

What do children know about information writing?

Today's children are surrounded by examples of different genres and formats of information writing. Food packets, tins and jars, for example, include text and tables of figures as well as artwork and photographs. Children see informational texts on TV (especially on teletext)

and computer screens. They hear news broadcasts, and may read newspapers. Family members may consult timetables, telephone directories, holiday brochures and TV guides. Children also know about information writing from their own reading of non-fiction books at home and in school.

FEATURES OF INFORMATIONAL TEXTS

1. What happened to me (recount). The purpose of recounting is to inform and/or entertain by linking facts through a narrative. Recounts are usually written in the past tense, and consist of
(a) A scene-setting opening (**orientation**), such as 'Yesterday I went to the park.'
(b) The recount of events as they occurred in sequence (**chronological order**), for example: 'I walked round the pond, then stopped to feed the ducks. Then I went to the swing park. After that I watched the boys playing cricket.'
(c) A closing statement (**re-orientation**), such as 'I like going to the park.'

Children will encounter and use recount mode in biographical and autobiographical accounts, in diaries and in letters. It is probably the easiest genre of information writing for young children to tackle, because it so closely resembles spoken language.

2. How things are (report). In a report, the writer organises relevant information into a chosen structure. Reports describe the way something is. The purpose of a report is to organise and store factual information on a topic. In general, reports:
• are written in the present tense;
• do not include personal information or opinions;
• should be accurate, clear and concise;
• may use technical terms or specialised vocabulary.

A report usually has an opening, including some classification of the subject (for example, 'Dogs are animals'); followed by a description of the subject, referring to various aspects of it (for example, 'Dogs make good pets. Some dogs are fluffy and cuddly. Others are useful for keeping you safe. Some dogs help to guide blind people. Most dogs like walking, sleeping and eating dog food.')

Young children generally use the report mode when gathering information on a subject. **Description** is an important element in reports, and may take the form of drawings or photographs as well as text.

3. Why things happen (explanation). In an explanation, the writer describes a process or how something works. Explanations are usually written in the present tense. They include action clauses, and use temporal or causal connections.
Explanations usually have:
1. A general statement to introduce the topic – for example, 'This is how LEGO works.'
2. A series of logical steps explaining how or why something (the subject) occurs – for example, 'Each LEGO brick has a pattern of studs on top and holes underneath. These are arranged so that any brick can be fixed onto another brick either lengthways or sideways. It will stay fixed when other bricks are added, but can easily be pulled off.'

The explanations given by children aged 5 to 7 are likely to be descriptive rather than offer causes and reasons for events. While logical description of a sequence of events is an important step towards explanation, the teacher should also encourage the child to look at 'Why?/Because' relationships.

It is also important to distinguish between explanations and instructions. An explanation tells us how something works or is done, while an instruction tells us how to do something.

HOW A SWITCH WORKS

HOW A LIGHT BULB WORKS

TEACHING INFORMATION WRITING

The national curricula for England and Wales, Scotland and Northern Ireland require that children learn to value writing as a means of remembering, communicating, organising and developing ideas. They should develop confidence in their handling of information by experiencing writing for a variety of practical purposes, for different audiences, using different layouts and formats. In brief, children should learn to recognise the following:

1. A written record of information or experience can be a memory aid.
2. Writing a personal account of an enjoyable or amusing experience shares the enjoyment with others as well as giving pleasure to the author.
3. Information writing can be used to follow up an interest in, and develop knowledge of, a wide variety of subjects.
4. Knowledge of the different genres of information writing helps to develop awareness of the ways in which written information is provided in books, magazines, encyclopaedias and other reference works, and enhances reading skills.
5. Increasing familiarity with information books helps to create awareness of their structural features, such as contents lists, headings, captions, glossary and index.

What it takes

To be successful information writers, children need to
• be clear about their purpose and audience;
• be able to select key ideas;
• organise and/or sequence information appropriately;
• find appropriate vocabulary (which may be technical);
• include appropriate illustrations (drawings, diagrams, photographs);
• select the most appropriate format (diary, letter, programme, timetable and so on).

Children should also be encouraged to think about the criteria for a successful piece of information writing:
• getting it right (**accuracy**);
• saying it all (**comprehensiveness**);
• fitting it together (**coherence**);
• being clear (**clarity**);
• standing back (**objectivity**).

How can these skills be taught?

Information writing has long been a familiar part of primary project work in social subjects such as history, geography, science and health. Teachers often set writing tasks in order to develop children's knowledge and understanding of the content of the topic. Here the emphasis is on content: **writing to learn**. But children should also be introduced to the distinctive features and structures of information writing if they are to develop as writers. Here the emphasis is on the process: **learning to write**.

Both elements are important, but the teacher must be clear about the main focus of teaching for each task: *Is the main purpose to develop the child's understanding of the subject, or to develop the child's skill as a writer and communicator of ideas?* As far as possible, the teacher should develop information writing from children's interests and enthusiasms. It is necessary to take time to discover what these interests and enthusiasms are – by talking and listening to children, by observing their play, and by making contact with parents and family members.

Giving children opportunities to recount their personal experiences verbally helps them to prepare for creating drawn and written recounts. Introducing and discussing information books as part of the reading programme enables the teacher to draw attention to their structural features and to the style of writing adopted for giving information. Information books provide models which children can use to frame their first attempts at writing reports and explanations.

Contents of this chapter

The activities which follow are focused on two main aspects of information writing:
• **reading to find things out** (features of information books – contents pages, glossaries, indexes and so on);
• **writing to tell people things** (selecting key ideas, wording, awareness of purpose and audience).

Activity	Teaching content	Star rating	Group size	Photo-copiable
1 The weather today	Giving information in a report in short, clear statements.	**/***	Ⓦ ⇨ 1	✓
2 Hobbies Factfile	Structuring information in concise form as a 'factfile'.	**/***	Ⓦ ⇨ 4 ⇨ 1	✓✓
3 Cool clothes	Organising and presenting information in visual form with descriptive text.	**/***	4 ⇨ Ⓦ ⇨ 2	✓✓
4 Find the facts	Finding the main ideas in a text, selecting and reporting.	***	6 ⇨ 1	✓✓
5 A letter from Calum	Recounting an event in a letter format and creating a reply.	*	Ⓦ ⇨ 1	✓✓
6 Something precious	Giving clear and concise information on a personal topic.	**	Ⓦ ⇨ 2 ⇨ 1	✓✓
7 What I did at school today	Creating a personal recount based on experience within a time sequence.	*	Ⓦ ⇨ 1	✓
8 Baby Bear has his say	Recounting from the point of view of a character in a well-known story.	*	4	✓
9 Read the label	Locating information on a label. Creating a similar label.	***	8 ⇨ 2	✓✓
10 My favourite sandwich	Recording information in a pictograph and interpreting the results.	*	Ⓦ ⇨ 1 ⇨ Ⓦ	✓
11 What is a glossary?	Recognising the function of a glossary and why it is useful.	***	Ⓦ ⇨ 2	✓
12 Can you explain why?	Giving a simple explanation of why something is as it is.	*/**	Ⓦ ⇨ 1	✓
13 What's in the leaflet?	What makes a good leaflet – examining the structure of the information.	***	Ⓦ ⇨ 2 ⇨ 6 ⇨ Ⓦ	✓
14 Designing a leaflet	Structuring your own leaflet: writing to tell people about something.	***	Ⓦ ⇨ 2 ⇨ Ⓦ	✓
15 All about us	Selecting information about a subject. Deciding on headings. Creating a contents page.	**	4 ⇨ Ⓦ	✓
16 How I made this model	Writing a recount with accuracy and detail. Illustrating the text.	**/**/***	4	✓
17 Classroom Newsdesk	Recounting and recording play events as a news report.	*/**	Ⓦ ⇨ 4 ⇨ 1	✓
18 We need a class noticeboard	Organising and using a noticeboard.	*/**/***	Ⓦ ⇨ 4 ⇨ 1	
19 Classroom calendar	Noting key events in a sequence using a calendar format.	*/**/***	Ⓦ ⇨ 1	✓
20 Happy Something To You	Designing an appropriate greeting card for a particular person and occasion.	*/**	Ⓦ ⇨ 4 ⇨ 1	✓

Ⓦ = whole class

THE WEATHER TODAY

Teaching content

In a report, information is given in short, clear statements.

What you need

A weather poster or information book; sample weather reports from newspapers; copies of photocopiable page 49 (also enlarged copy), writing materials.

What to do

Gather the whole class together to look at the weather poster (or information books), asking them what information it gives. Their answers should include different types of weather (for example: when it is sunny, cloudy, raining, snowing) as well as wind speed and direction.

Read out a weather report or forecast from the newspaper, encouraging the children to identify and discuss:

1. What information it gives – for example, what the weather was/will be like in the morning, afternoon, evening; weather in different parts of the country; how the weather changes or moves across the country.

2. How the information is given – short, clear statements such as:

- 'Rain in all parts by 6 o'clock.'
- 'Winds light, south-westerly…'

Ask the children to recall yesterday's weather. Build up a report with them, using an enlarged version of photocopiable page 49. Emphasise the need to use short, clear statements and phrases, for example:

Morning: Cloudy with some sunny intervals.
Afternoon: Rain at times.
Evening: Heavy showers and high winds.

Remind the children that this is a report of what happened. Ask them to explain how a forecast is different. Is the language used different? Complete the modelling by asking pupils to make a forecast of the weather for tomorrow. (They could base it on the current weather.) For example,

The forecast for tomorrow is: Wind dropping, clear skies, sunny.

Give each child a copy of page 49. This can be used in different ways;

- the children drawing and the teacher scribing;
- the children drawing and writing;
- the children writing.

Explain that at some point during the morning and the afternoon they should record what the weather is like; then they should take the sheet home to complete their evening report and to make a forecast for tomorrow, based on listening to or watching a weather forecast on radio or TV.

The children's reports and forecasts can be shared on the following day, then compared and contrasted. Discuss effective wording and pictures. The forecasts can be tested against the actual weather. Were they accurate?

HOBBIES FACTFILE

Teaching content

Writing which gives information should be organised, clear, concise and relevant. The 'factfile' format satisfies these criteria.

What you need

Large blank sheets of newsprint, marker pens; copies of photocopiable pages 50 and 51, writing materials.

What to do

Many children enjoy compiling factfiles on a variety of subjects which interest them: football, school, TV programmes, friends, and so on. Figure 1 shows an example of a personal factfile.* Explain to the class that they will create factfiles for their own hobbies or interests.

Figure 1

MY PERSONAL FOOTBALL FACT FILE

Name: Calum Lindsay
Age: 6
School: Glendale
Best foot: Left
Best position: in goal
Teams played for: Manchester
Utd Kids

My team's strip: red

The best match I've played in Scotland
v England

Favourite football team England

Nickname Gazza

Favourite team's strip: (home) red

(away) yellow + red blue + white
Ground: Old Trafford
Best player: Cantona
Worst player: Cooke
Favourite match: Man Utd v Nottingham
First match I went to: M Utd v N Forest
Man Utd 5 Score: Nots Forest 0
If I were manager of my country's
football team, I would pick this side:
1. Gazza   2. Southgate
3. Sheringham   4. Ince
5. Adams   6. Platt
7. G. Neville   8. Jones
9. P. Nevile   10. M. Manaman
11. Palister

Organise the class into groups of four to six children. Ask each group to consider what information they would include in a personal hobby factfile. What facts do they think are important to tell people? The children should list these facts on a large sheet of newsprint. The lists should then be brought together so that the children can look for similarities and differences. Try to pull out the key elements from each list, such as:

• what the hobby is;
• what you need to do it (equipment, special clothing);
• when the child first started the hobby;
• what the child likes best and least about it.

Introduce and explain photocopiable sheets 50 and 51. The children can go on to complete these individually. If they want to substitute any of their own ideas for those included on the sheets, they should be encouraged to do so.

Further development

The finished sheets could form the first two pages of a more extended factfile on hobbies. * The Football Factfile is taken from *The Fantastic Football Fun Book* by Alan Durant, illustrated by Cathy Gale (Walker Books Ltd, 1996).

3

COOL CLOTHES

✱✱✱✱✱ ††††→ⓦ→†† 60

Teaching content

How to organise and present the relevant information clearly and succinctly, using pictures and descriptive text.

What you need

Pages from clothes catalogues with pictures, descriptions and prices; photocopiable pages 52 (cut into cards) and 53, writing materials; a chalkboard or large sheet of paper.

What to do

Organise the class into groups of four to six children. Give each group an occasion card cut from a copy of page 52. Ask them to look through the catalogue pages to find a suitable outfit for the occasion.

When they have chosen, ask them to show the other children what they have chosen and to explain why. Ask the groups also to explain how they found the information they needed. List their ideas on a chalkboard or large sheet of paper – looking at the pictures, reading the descriptions and so on.

Explore with the class whether or not the pictures would be enough.
• *What does the written description add?*
• *What kind of information is given in the words?*

Make a new list detailing information provided under various headings, such as:

colour

size (eg size 8 or small/medium/large)

length (eg for skirt or trousers)

material

washing instructions

fastenings

age range

price

Display this list for the children's later use.

Organise the children into pairs, making sure that each pair has an occasion card. Explain that their task is to create and design an outfit for the occasion they have been given, drawing suitable clothes, and to write a description of their outfit giving all the necessary information. The list above will help them to structure their information. If some children need additional support, these headings could be added to the 'Ideal for...' photocopiable page.

Give each pair a copy of the 'Ideal for...' photocopiable sheet (page 53). They should design the outfit (by drawing, making a collage or another method) on the left-hand side of the page and describe it on the right-hand side.

The completed sheets can be brought together to create a *Cool Clothes Catalogue*.

FIND THE FACTS

Teaching content
Finding information in a book, using the index and contents page. Passing on this information clearly in writing to other people.

What you need
A selection of information books linked to the current class topic (such as books giving facts about aeroplanes or dinosaurs); photocopiable pages 54 and 55, writing materials.

What to do
This activity is designed as a group task, which could be introduced to the class gradually (one group at a time) over one to two weeks. It can be adapted for use with various non-fiction titles, and is probably best linked to the current class topic. Each group is allocated, or chooses, one topic from a list supplied by the teacher. For example, a book about dinosaurs might lend itself to such topics as: When they lived, Where they lived, What they ate, What they looked like.

Working with the group, introduce the 'Information sheet' (photocopiable page 55). Explain that they will use this to record **four** important facts about their topic which can be shared with other groups.

Give out copies of the 'Finding the facts' sheet (photocopiable page 54) and model the procedure for one fact (not the group's):
• How would we go about finding books on this topic? (From key words in title, from area of library.) Note down the title, author and publisher on the information sheet.
• Where is the contents page usually located? What does it tell us?
• Where is the index? How do we use it?

Children can suggest relevant page numbers and note these on scrap paper, then look up these pages to locate information which they also note down on scrap paper. Working as a group, they then complete the information sheet before going on to work individually on their own fact-finding mission.

This work establishes the practice of noting information down in rough form while searching through reference materials, then writing it up in a neat, organised form at the end.

Frogs live in water

Frogs are good at jumping

Frogs have big round eyes

Frogs grow from tadpoles

When all the groups have completed their information sheets, each group should report to the class. The information sheets can be made into a book of useful facts.

Further development

Encourage children to use the 'Finding the facts' sheet and the information sheet to start factfiles about topics that interest them. Link this activity to information books which you have available in the class or school library. Children who enjoy searching for facts might like to compile their own book or folder, such as *Four Facts About Frogs*.

5

A LETTER FROM CALUM

Teaching content

Recounting events in a sequence using 'first', 'then' and 'finally', in a letter format.

What you need

Calum's letter (photocopiable page 56) in an envelope addressed to the class; other copies or an enlarged/OHT version of page 56; word cards saying **first**, **then**, **finally**; photocopiable page 57, writing materials.

What to do

Ask someone in school to deliver the letter to the class. Select a child to open the envelope and read the letter aloud. Then ask:
- *Why has Calum written to us?*
- *What did he have to tell us?*

Explain to the children that a letter is a good way of telling people what has happened to you. Look at Calum's letter in detail (giving a copy to each child, or using a poster-sized or OHT version), or read it again. Then ask the children: *Can you remember what happened...*
- *first?*
Calum fell from a high climbing frame.
- *then?*
He went to hospital and had an X-ray.
- *finally?*
He got a present from his sister.

You may wish to go over this again, drawing children's attention to the key words for sequencing. Show the three word cards and pin them to the wall.

Tell the children that they are going to write back to Calum, to cheer him up by telling him about something that has happened to them. Discuss possibilities – maybe they also had an accident, or went on a trip, or went to a party.

Introduce the 'Dear Calum' sheet (photocopiable page 57) and read it out to the children. Explain that they can draw what happened **first**, **then** and **finally** in the boxes and write what happened if they can. If they need help, you will scribe for them.

Completed letters to Calum could be displayed in the classroom, with suitably addressed envelopes.

SOMETHING PRECIOUS

** ⟶ W ⟶ ††† (60)

Teaching content

Giving information clearly and concisely about a valued possession.

What you need

Your own 'precious' object in a decorated box; photocopiable pages xxx and xxx, writing materials; a chalkboard or large sheet of paper.

What to do

Gather the class closely around you. Explain that you have brought something which is precious to you for them to see. It is in a decorated box. Stress that 'precious' does not necessarily mean valuable in terms of money. Show them the box and ask whether anyone can guess what is inside. After a few guesses, ask the children how they could find out more about the precious object **without** opening the box. Elicit the response they could ask questions of you. Encourage the children to think about the kind of questions which could help them find out both what the object is and why it is precious – for example:

- *What does it feel like?*
- *What does it look like?*
- *What colour is it?*
- *What size is it?*
- *Can you wear it, play with it, cuddle it?*
- *Do you use it to do something?*
- *Where did it come from?*
- *Was it a gift? Who gave it to you?*
- *Have you had it for a long time?*

The children will begin to get a picture of what the object is and why it is precious to you. Recap the main points with them, scribing on a chalkboard or a large sheet of paper. For example:

- It is small.
- It is black with shining jewelled eyes.
- It has four legs.
- It sits on my shelf.

Now ask the children: *What is it?* They may succeed in guessing:

- It's a cat ornament.

Explain that *It's precious to me because:*

- I've had it for five years.
- It was a Christmas present from my daughter when she was four.
- It makes me feel happy and loved.

Ask the children to think of an object that is precious to them. They must not tell anyone, but keep it a secret for now. This activity needs to be handled sensitively to allow for children's different feelings about what is 'precious'.

Organise the children into pairs. Issue one 'Questions about your precious object' sheet (photocopiable page 58) to each pair. One partner acts as questioner. The other gives answers. When they have worked through the questions, the pair swap roles and start again.

Stress that the answers should be short but accurate, and should tell the partners what they want to know. When both partners have had a turn, ask for some feedback. 'Were you able to find out what the precious object was?'

Finally, give out and explain the 'My precious object' sheet (photocopiable page 59). Ask the children to complete this sheet individually. The completed sheets could be displayed with photographs, drawings or models or be compiled as a group or class book. Individual children might like to make a small book about several things that are precious to them.

7

WHAT I DID AT SCHOOL TODAY

* ▭ Ⓦ→╁ ⏱40

Teaching content

Creating a personal recount based on experience within a time sequence.

What you need

Photocopiable page 60, writing materials; an A3 copy of page 60 with three pictures of what the teacher did earlier in the day.

What to do

This activity works best at the end of the school day, and provides an opportunity for children to recount what they have done. You may wish to choose a day when there is a TV programme, a PE lesson or a visit to provide some specific events for younger children to recount.

Talk with the class about some of the things they have been involved in during the day. Break this down into more specific time units: before/after playtime and lunchtime. Explain to the children that they are going to draw some pictures to help them tell everyone at home what they have done today.

Model this for the children, using the flow diagram on photocopiable page 60 enlarged to A3 size (without the title) so that they can all see it. Start by drawing (or have drawn in advance) **what you did** (at school) first thing in the morning, and write a caption to accompany your drawing in the space provided underneath. Repeat for the next two boxes of the flow diagram, so that your recount looks something like Figure 2.

Ask the children to suggest a title – such as *My day at school*, *What I did at school today*, or *Monday at school*. Each child should write her/his name at the top, as author.

Now ask the children to think of any three things they have done that day and start to draw the first thing in box 1. They should use the three boxes to show a sequence of events. You may have to scribe for some children, or supply particular written words.

Finally, gather the class together again and select a few children to read their recount of the day's events to the rest of the class. The children take their own recounts home to be read to their families.

Further development

The activity could be done over the course of a week, using a zigzag book with one page per day. Children could also be encouraged to write a recount (in pictures and captions) of what they did at the weekend to bring to school on Monday.

First I said, "Good morning".

Next I told a story.

Then I took everyone outside to see the leaves.

Figure 2

8

BABY BEAR HAS HIS SAY

* ▭ †††† ⊙40

Teaching content

Recounting from the point of view of a character in a well-known story.

What you need

A play situation in which the story can be enacted (such as the Three Bears' Cottage); puppets or a flannelgraph; photocopiable page 61; newspaper, glue; writing and drawing materials.

What to do

To introduce this activity, give children the opportunity to role play the Goldilocks story through a structured play situation, using puppets or a flannelgraph. The activity which follows may be best organised during a Choosing Time or Structured Activity Time, when others in the class are also involved in play situations. Allocate a group of four children to this task and explain that each child must choose to be either Daddy Bear, Mummy Bear, Baby Bear or Goldilocks.

To help model the process, it would be useful for you to take on the role of a newspaper reporter. When the children have finished the role play, step in and explain that you have come to hear Baby Bear's side of the story because he always looks sad in pictures.

Gather the group round a table and begin by asking the child playing Baby Bear if he/she can explain what happened in his/her own words. You will write down the story for your newspaper. Prompt with some questions as necessary.

• *Baby Bear, can I take you right back to first thing this morning in your cottage? What was happening then?*
• *So you went out? Did you leave the door open? Did you ever imagine that anyone might break in?*
• *What did you see when you first opened the door?*
• *What was the last thing to happen?*

As the dialogue progresses, write text in each of the four boxes on photocopiable page 61 to cover the main episodes. (Write next to the number in each box.) Elicit comments from the other bears, corroborating or adding to Baby Bear's story. Model the use of 'I' (Baby Bear) or 'We' (the Bears) the whole way through, using the children's words as far as possible. At the end, read out the story and ask Baby Bear whether it is a true account.

Finally, cut out the boxes on a blank copy of page 61 and allocate one to each child in the group. Ask them to draw a picture (in the small box) to accompany the words. When the pictures are completed, the group can stick them in order onto a newspaper background with the title *Baby Bear's Story*.

READ THE LABEL

*** ††††·†† ⑮

Teaching content

Locating information on a label. Creating a label which communicates facts.

What you need

Photocopiable pages 62 and 63, blank sheets of A4 paper (one per pair); a shirt, a dress, a pair of trousers, a pair of trainers or shoes; a large sheet of paper; pencils, thin black felt pens; adhesive (suitable for fabric and paper).

What to do

Start with a group of eight children. Set the context for the activity by showing them the various items of clothing which you have brought in (see above). Divide the group into pairs. Tell the children that you want them to find the labels on these clothes and to talk to each other about the different types of information they find on the labels. When they have had enough time to do this, collate their findings on a large sheet of paper headed 'Labels give us information about ...'

Information found on a clothing label will vary, but it should tell you about:

- the size;
- the type of clothing;
- where it was made;
- washing instructions;
- ironing instructions;
- the manufacturer or shop;
- the designer's logo/name;
- the type of fabric.

Now look at the label on photocopiable page 63. Give out copies of the sheet, and ask the children to compare it with the list which they have generated. Draw their attention to the way in which the information on the sheet has been written in a shorthand form, with the use of signs. Ask why they think it is written in this way. How do the makers decide which is the most important information to put in the limited space?

Now tell the children that they must work in pairs to design a label for a T-shirt. They have to think about who will read it, what facts are necessary and how these facts will be written. Hand out the blank sheets of A4 paper. On one half of the blank sheet, the pair should make a draft copy of their label in pencil; on the other half, they should then make a final copy in black felt pen.

Using photocopiable sheet 62, each pair should then design the front of a T-shirt. Ask them to take the final copy of the label, cut it out and stick it onto the photocopiable sheet in the box provided. Finally, ask each pair to list the information which their label gives in the last box on the sheet.

Display the completed sheets for other children to read, or collate them in a class book of clothing labels to which other examples may be added at a later date.

MY FAVOURITE SANDWICH

Teaching content

Recording information in the form of a pictograph and interpreting the results.

What you need

Photocopiable sheet 64, three large sheets of paper (one for tallying, one for the pictograph, one to record conclusions), coloured pencils.

What to do

This activity could be linked to a topic on food; it can also stand on its own as a relevant context for handling information, providing an opportunity for young children to talk about the process of gathering information.

Start by asking the children to close their eyes and think of their favourite sandwich. If they could choose any sandwich filling for lunch, what would it be? You may have to be prepared for very individual tastes. Choose one child and ask her/him to tell you her/his favourite sandwich filling (for example, tuna). Record this on a large sheet of paper and ask whether anyone else had decided on this as a favourite. For each additional vote, mark a tick on the large sheet of paper beside the word 'tuna'. Continue with this process until all choices have been recorded. Ask the children to look at the large sheet and tell you what information this gives (types of sandwich filling, number of people who like each one). There may even be an obvious favourite.

Now explain that they are going to draw a picture of their choice of sandwich, to form part of a graph which will make the information even clearer. As the children go back to their seats, remind them to stick to their original choice – they can't change their minds now! Hand out one sandwich picture from photocopiable sheet 64 to each child, and ask them to draw/colour in the filling. This should not take long. Meanwhile, prepare a large scale for a pictograph, with a line for each sandwich filling (see Figure 3).

Select one of the sandwich fillings and ask all the children who have drawn this filling to come to the front of the class and stick their picture on the appropriate line. You will have to watch this to check that the information is being placed accurately. When these children have placed their pictures, they should sit down at the front of the class. Repeat this until the complete graph has been built up (all the children have added their pictures).

Finally, ask the children what the graph tells them. Record this on a large sheet of paper to put beside the graph. Figure 4 shows the kind of information that should be recorded.

The children could repeat this activity in a different context, such as favourite sports.

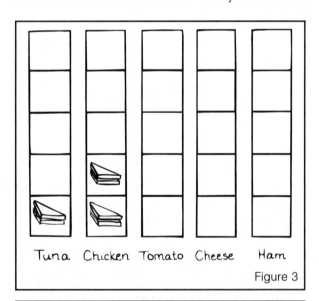

Tuna   Chicken   Tomato   Cheese   Ham

Figure 3

Our graph tells us:

We like different fillings.

The favourite is _____

The same number of children like _____ and _____

_____ children like cheese.

No-one likes _____

More children like _____ than _____

Figure 4

11

WHAT IS A GLOSSARY?

✱✱✱ Ⓦ→†† 🕘30

Teaching content
Recognising the function of a glossary and why it is useful.

What you need
At least two examples of information books with glossaries; photocopiable page 65; pens or pencils.

What to do
Start by talking with the whole class about books which give information about various subjects. Show them two (or more) which have a glossary, and explain that this feature is often found at the back of an information book. Ask the children whether they have seen a glossary before. Point to the relevant pages and ask them to look first of all at the print: what do they notice? The key words will usually be in bold or italic lettering, with the explanation of the term in plain text.

Look at one or two examples and encourage the children to tell you what they think the purpose of a glossary may be. Make sure that they understand that a glossary will give an explanation of a word or offer another word

with the same meaning. Give the children some examples of explanations and ask them to suggest which words they might explain:
• A group of children taught together.
• Worn to keep hands warm.
Then ask the children to give explanations for:
• nose
• house
• chalkboard.
Organise the children to work in pairs. Give each pair a copy of photocopiable page 65 and explain that all of the words and meanings in this glossary have been mixed up. Can they match the words to the correct explanations? At the foot of the sheet, they should write a sentence to explain 'rain' and guess which word is being explained in the last box.

Further development
Ask the children to create a glossary for their current topic.

12

CAN YOU EXPLAIN WHY?

✱✱✱ Ⓦ→† 🕘40

Teaching content
Giving a simple explanation of why something is as it is.

What you need
Photocopiable page 66; an enlarged (A3) copy of page 66; pens or pencils.

What to do
This activity presents children with familiar situations which they have to explain in response to a *Why?* question. Gather the class together and make sure they can all see the A3-sized copy of photocopiable page 66. Ask them to look at the first picture: *Can you explain to me what is happening here? Why is the boy wearing a bandage?*

Take some of the children's responses to the second question and record them in the space provided – for example, *He's wearing a bandage because he fell off his bike*, or *The nurse put a bandage on his leg to stop it bleeding.* Try to discourage children from starting their sentences with 'Because'.

Model another example with the children – for example, the spotty face could be explained as caused by measles or chickenpox.

Why did the cat climb the tree?

Why does it always rain on the day of the big match?

Why did the chicken cross the road?

Now hand out copies of photocopiable page 66; ask the children to write their explanations in the boxes under the pictures. To collate some of their work, you may choose to cut out some of the children's writing and display it under each of the large pictures on the A3 version. A class frieze could be entitled *We can explain why.*

Further development

To extend this activity, ask children to draw a picture and write a question beginning with *Why?* to accompany it. Children could work in pairs, exchange their pictures and write on appropriate explanations.

What to do

Set the scene for this activity by asking whether anyone in the class has ever visited a famous park or building. How did they find out about it? Ask children who have never been to one how they think they could find information about one. Try to elicit the response that often there are posters or leaflets which will give information about a place.

Show the class the leaflets which you have brought in. Explain that these usually come folded up; when opened out, they give you lots of different pieces of information.

Organise the class into pairs. Tell the children that each pair will look through the leaflet and record some of the information on the photocopiable sheet. Give each pair a leaflet and a copy of photocopiable page 67. Explain that you want them to:
• find out the name of the place;
• list the things visitors can do there;
• note any other interesting information;
• write down three things that make this a good leaflet (consider pictures, layout, captions, logo and so on).

The children will need some time for this initial part of the activity. Your role will be to discuss the task with the pairs and assist with the recording process.

Stop the activity at an appropriate moment, and explain that the pairs are now going to work together in groups of six to produce a large record sheet which collates the information under the headings: *Things to do; Other information; What makes it a good leaflet?*

13

WHAT'S IN THE LEAFLET?

Teaching content

What makes a good leaflet – examining the structure of the information.

What you need

A selection of leaflets (one per pair of children) advertising a place to visit (such as a National Trust park or building, or a theme park); one copy per pair of photocopiable page 67; one large sheet of paper per group, perhaps with headings written as on page 67; pens or pencils; a highlighter pen.

Appoint one child in each group to scribe. Hand out a large sheet of paper to each group. It may help to have the headings already written on.

Finally, bring the whole class together. Using a highlighter pen, identify the key points which make a useful and informative leaflet. Leave the children's large record sheets on display, to be referred to in the 'Designing a leaflet' activity (see below).

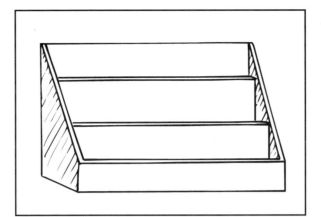

14
DESIGNING A LEAFLET

Teaching content
Structuring your own leaflet: writing to tell people about something.

What you need
A4 blank paper; children's work from the 'What's in the leaflet?' activity (see above); a variety of leaflets; pencils, coloured pencils and pens.

What to do
Start by reviewing some of the key features of a good leaflet (for a place to visit) identified in the previous activity, 'What's in the leaflet?'
• Clear information.
• A variety of things to do.
• Opening times, prices, phone numbers.
• Special events.
• Layout, print, words used.
• A map showing how to get there.

Now explain to the children that they are going to work in the same pairs to design a leaflet to tell other people about a place. You may decide on the context for this, or allow them to choose: a theme park, zoo, safari park, museum, sports centre, shopping centre or place linked to the class topic. A variety of leaflets would be useful to suggest ideas for context and style, though the children should not be encouraged simply to copy. Before they start, show them how the leaflet can be constructed by folding a sheet of A4 paper in half or into three equal sections.

The design of the children's own leaflet may take some time. They should make a pencilled draft first, using their 'checklists' (the large record sheets) from the 'What's in the leaflet?' activity, and then make a final version using pens and colouring in.

The finished leaflets should be presented to the whole class. They could then be displayed in a special information box. (See illustration.)

15
ALL ABOUT US

Teaching content
To create an 'all about' book a writer selects information about a subject, decides on headings and creates a contents page.

What you need
One folded or zigzag book with A4 pages (the number of pages will depend on what each group decides, but three to six double-page spreads should be enough) and one published information book per group; writing and drawing materials; photocopiable page 68; scissors, adhesive.

What to do

This activity is a 'mini-project' which draws together various ideas about structure and layout by requiring children to create their own information booklets. One appropriate context for creating these booklets might be if the class were linked to a school in another part of the UK or abroad. Alternatively, this activity could be linked to the project 'Please visit our class' in the Key Stage 1 *Non-Fiction Writing Projects* book, or to the arrival of a new headteacher or a new pupil.

A few days in advance, discuss the context (see above) to establish the audience for the writing. Then tell the children that each group will be working to produce a booklet called 'All About Us'. Ask them to think about what they would want to tell people about themselves – for example *my name, what I look like, where I live, my family, our pets, what I like to do at home and at school, things I am good at* – and to look for any useful material (such as photographs, newspaper cuttings and personal items) which could go into a booklet.

Divide the class into groups of four to six children. Show them a blank folder or zigzag booklet. Remind the children that their booklet is to be about **them**: the members of their group. Tell them that it should contain text and illustrations. Use some published information books (one for each group) to remind the children of the layout sequence: cover with title, illustration and author; contents page; information pages; glossary (if present) and index. Ask the children to suggest what they

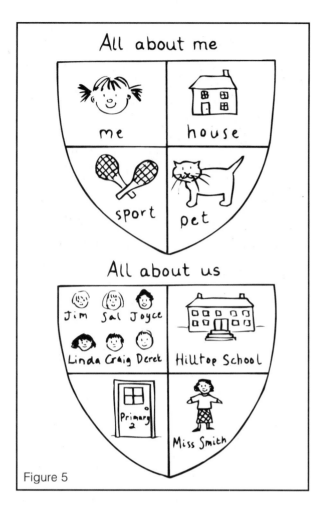

Figure 5

need to do first, and discuss their ideas and reasons. Work towards an agreement that starting with the contents list will help the writer to decide what information to include (and also that the glossary, index, cover and title can be done much later).

Now ask the class for some suggestions about the contents of the booklet: *What could you tell people about yourselves? What do you think they would want to know?* List some ideas on a chalkboard or a large sheet of paper, then ask the groups to discuss among themselves and fill in photocopiable page 68 to show their proposed list of contents. This might be along the following lines:
- **Who we are** (photographs or self-portraits with full names and dates of birth);
- **Where we live** (drawings of houses, gardens);
- **In our families** (photos or drawings of parents and siblings);
- **Pets we own**;
- **Favourite foods**;
- **Sports and hobbies**;
- **School work**;
- **Trips and holidays**; and so on.

Each group reports back, so that ideas can be shared and lists amended. However, the groups

4 Mill Close

Flat 2
25 Church Road

49 Sunnyside Park

117 Selby Heights

should follow their own interests and create different contents lists.

Future sessions can allow the children, working as individuals and in co-operation with other group members, to create pages for their books by writing, drawing, cutting and sticking. Each day, the group could tackle a new heading from their contents list, generating material, collating it into a layout and then completing the page or pages. When all the 'chapters' have been compiled, the group can decide whether a glossary is required, number the pages, create an index and put page numbers on their contents page. Finally, a cover with a title, the authors' names and a suitable illustration should be created, perhaps using the coat of arms/quadrant idea illustrated in Figure 5.

The number of sessions needed for this work will depend on what contents the children have decided to provide. For younger children, it might be best to contain the entire 'mini-project' within a week's work. Older children could be given more time.

Completed booklets should be shared in class before they are given or sent to the intended audience. Hopefully, those who receive the books will write back with thanks and comments.

Note: For younger classes, it may be easier for individual children to make a very simple zigzag booklet called 'All About Me'. Each page could have one illustration (a drawing or photo) with a one-word or one-line caption.

HOW I MADE THIS MODEL

✳✳✳✳✳ ⁓⁓⁓⁓ 30

Teaching content

Writing a recount of a model-making activity requires accurate detail. Photographs, drawings and diagrams can be used to illustrate the text.

What you need

Models recently made by the children; samples of materials and tools used; writing paper, pencils or pens; photocopiable page 69; a writing table.

What to do

The children should recently have made models from junk materials. While this writing activity develops naturally from oral recounting of practical activities in choosing times or structured play sessions, the question of purpose and audience still needs to be addressed. In this case, the children could be writing for their parents and grandparents or for the headteacher. It is important that the audience is 'distant', because that demands a higher level of accuracy and detail.

Gather a group of four to eight children at the writing table. Each child should have her/his model and a blank card to make a label for it. First, ask each child to tell the group what her/his model is and to write the name on the caption card.

Tell the children that they are going to write about their models for their parents or carers, or for the headteacher. What do they think their audience might want to know? Discuss their ideas to establish a simple frame which answers the questions: 'What is your model?' and 'How did you make it?' Tell the children the second question needs thinking about: their models may have taken a long time to make, have many different parts, and so on. Let some children explain orally. Then ask each child to think about the three main steps: *How I began/What I did first, How I went on/What I did next, What I did last/How I finished*. Also, remind the children that their audience was/were not here to see what happened. 'You need to tell them *everything* – exactly!' Discuss with the group whether drawings (or diagrams) would help.

Give the children a copy each of photocopiable page 69. Explain or discuss it if necessary, then leave them to work on it. When they have finished, sheets can be exchanged. The reader of each sheet may comment and ask the writer questions. More writing may be required before the recounts are ready to be taken home or sent to the headteacher. Remember to ask the readers to give feedback to the writers.

Further development

The theme of 'What I can do at school' can provide opportunities for a variety of recounts which are based on pupils' classroom experiences – for example, *I can play with sand/water; I can water the plants; I can go to the gym*. Send the written recounts home one at a time, or let the children compile a small booklet. This could be part of a larger project, such as 'Please visit our class' (see the Key Stage 1 *Non-Fiction Writing Projects* book).

CLASSROOM NEWSDESK

Teaching content

Recounting and recording of play events through developing role play as media reporters and photographers. Increased awareness of the onlooker's view. Selecting ideas to record and share with others.

What you need

An ongoing range of structured play activities or classroom and school events; materials to support role play as reporters and photographers (for example, reporters' notebooks and pens, a portable tape recorder and microphone, an easy-to-use camera with film, a table with a telephone, a typewriter, a noticeboard); writing materials; photocopiable page 70; examples of actual newspapers. If available, the computer could be used for word-processing.

What to do

Gather the class together, remarking that you are delighted to see so many interesting things happening during the choosing times. Give a few examples such as: a baby being taken ill in the house corner; the completion of an extra tall tower in the construction area; major works of art being produced by painters. Tell the children that, because of this, you are going to offer a new play opportunity: taking on the role of a newspaper, radio or TV reporter.

Discuss with the children what a reporter does, and what she/he needs to do her/his job. For example:

The reporter goes around looking for news stories. She observes events and writes about them, asks people questions and holds interviews. A reporter has a notepad and pencil, or a microphone and tape recorder. (Provide the appropriate equipment.) *Sometimes the reporter will take a photographer along to take pictures.* (These could be drawings or real photos. A Polaroid camera gives instant results, but is expensive to run. It might be better to have a simple camera using regular print film which can be processed within 24 hours.)

The reporters and photographers will require a base: the Newsdesk. Discuss with the children how this could be set up, using a table with a telephone, a typewriter or computer, a noticeboard and so on. Explain that there are opportunities for four children to play roles (two reporters and two photographers). Anyone can play, but they must be ready to share their reports with others. Introduce photocopiable page 70 and tell the children that they can use this for their newsdesk reports. Written reports will be 'published' on the class noticeboard; or,

if interest grows, a daily or weekly one-sheet newsletter might be printed and distributed.

Close the class discussion by telling the children that they can try this activity out at the next choosing time.

Later, offer the activity as part of choosing time. Use hats, armbands or badges to control numbers and assign roles. Two children can work at the newsdesk (see illustration) while another two are 'roving' in search of stories.

As the role play develops, the children should begin to generate a variety of written materials. The teacher's role is to develop and extend this through discussion and feedback, to encourage children to participate and sometimes to direct groups towards a special project – for example, the reporting team might be asked to 'cover' an in-school event such as sports day, or taken out to report on something happening in the community (such as a local flower show). Encourage the reporters to visit the house corner or class shop when exciting events (linked to play or a class topic) are taking place.

Foster the children's interest by encouraging them to look at reporting in newspapers and to listen to radio and TV reports. They could examine the layout and wording in newspaper reports to help them think of headlines for their own news stories.

Further development

From time to time, gather the class together to talk about the newsdesk activities and to suggest developments. 'Radio' reports could be made available on cassette through the listening unit, and 'TV' reports delivered 'on screen' (use an old TV set from which the back and tube have been removed, or make a set from a large cardboard box).

WE NEED A CLASS NOTICEBOARD

Teaching content
A noticeboard can be used to tell people about things or to make enquiries. Headings can be used to give different parts of the noticeboard different purposes and audiences. As space on a noticeboard is limited, notices should be brief and to the point.

What you need
A board or wall space in the classroom at an appropriate level for children's use; caption cards for headings; marker pens.

What to do
The context for this activity is everyday life in the classroom. A noticeboard can be used to assist communication, remind people about forthcoming events, draw attention to problems and so on. Setting up and using a noticeboard will provide opportunities for relevant, purposeful writing and reading by class members.

Ask the children to prepare for this activity by thinking about why a classroom noticeboard might be a good idea and how it might be used. Suggest that they look at noticeboards in the

school and other places (such as the supermarket, the church and the railway station) to see how these are organised and what sort of notices are displayed. Groups could be sent to look at the staffroom board, the headteacher's board, the school office board and the parents' board.

Gather the children together as a class to discuss their findings. List reasons for having a classroom noticeboard, and encourage the children to suggest what sort of notices should be displayed. Decide on the size and location of the noticeboard, then ask the children to suggest sections (for example: Wanted, Swop shop, Next week, Newsflash, Pick of the week, Pets' corner, Messages, URGENT) and allocate a space to each. Write headings and put them in place; inform the children that the noticeboard will be 'open' the next day.

If the children do not raise the question first, ask them to consider who will decide what goes on the noticeboard. Work towards agreeing that there could be an area for the teacher to use and an area for the class. Different groups or helpers should be responsible for different parts of the board. Look again at the headings and work out responsibilities with the children. Suggest that written 'rules' are needed, such as: *notices may be posted for one week only; new notices should be submitted on Monday for display from Wednesday*. List the children's ideas on a chalkboard or large sheet of paper, then select important and agreed ones.

To round off the initial session, each group has to write the first notice for its section. Discuss the purpose of a message or notice, the content and wording. How should it be designed to catch attention?

Use of the class noticeboard by groups and individuals should continue for several weeks (or for a term with older children). A box or file may be required for incoming notices. Two children could be appointed as helpers to sort these out and distribute them to groups responsible for different sections. Time should be allowed for writing notices and for sorting and display. Note that it may be helpful to have a 'free for all' section where anyone can put up any notice at any time. The noticeboard should be reviewed weekly to keep it 'alive'.

Further development
The teacher may wish to develop group functional writing activities linked to displays on the noticeboard, such as a poster about the opening of a sandwich shop, an advert for a super sandwich, a 'Save This Tree' slogan and so on.

CLASSROOM CALENDAR

Teaching content

The calendar format shows a month or year at a glance. The format allows key future events to be noted quickly and easily.

What you need

A large-scale calendar or wall planner, showing 12 months (each month space may be divided into weeks or days), marker pens in different colours, coloured stickers; photocopiable page 71, writing materials.

What to do

Note: If you are working with a Reception/P1 class, wait until after the Christmas holidays and use a calendar with a January to December layout; with an older class, introduce the calendar near the beginning of the school year and use one with an 'academic year' layout. The level of detail on the calendar (months, weeks or days) will affect the level of difficulty of the activity.

Gather the class together and introduce the large-scale calendar you have obtained or prepared, saying that the headteacher has sent this to the class as she/he thinks they might find it useful. Let the children look at it; check that they recognise what it is and what timescale it represents. Confirm that they know what year it is, and (if they are using an academic year layout) what year it will be in January. Write the

year(s) on the calendar if necessary.

Now ask the children to suggest useful, relevant information that should be recorded on the calendar. What future dates do they need to remember? Either write these directly or list the ideas suggested for later transfer. Suggestions might include:

- birthdays;
- festivals;
- school holidays;
- school and community events.

Children could contribute to the classroom calendar by writing their names for birthdays and making drawings for festivals. School holidays could be identified by using coloured stickers.

Now the children, working individually, should each make a calendar to keep in their personal folder. Photocopiable page 71 can be used to provide a 12-space frame. The children can write in the names of the months, illustrate the calendar and enter such information as they choose.

The large-scale calendar should be displayed in the classroom (perhaps on the noticeboard) to provide an 'events guide' and planner. New data should be added as appropriate. The calendar might also be used as a way of communicating messages (such as 'Remember to bring PE kit' or 'Money for outing today, please!') from teacher to children, children to teacher or children to children.

Further development

The children should continue with their personal calendars. These could be extended to become diaries, with notes and comments on events as they happen.

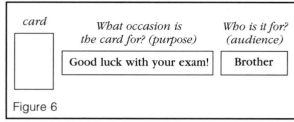

card	What occasion is the card for? (purpose)	Who is it for? (audience)
	Good luck with your exam!	Brother

Figure 6

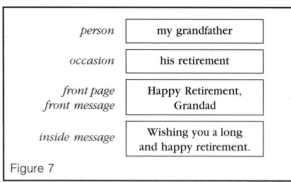

person	my grandfather
occasion	his retirement
front page front message	Happy Retirement, Grandad
inside message	Wishing you a long and happy retirement.

Figure 7

20

HAPPY SOMETHING TO YOU

Teaching content

Greetings cards are used to send messages. The message relates to an occasion which dictates the purpose and audience. The intended audience influences the message, design and style of the card.

What you need

A variety of greetings cards for different people and occasions (such as: birthday cards; congratulations cards for exam, driving test, new baby; Jewish New Year, Eid, Christmas and Easter cards; 'Good luck in your new job', 'Best wishes for your retirement' cards; Mother's Day, wedding and anniversary cards); strips of paper, large crayons or marker pens; photocopiable page 72, writing and drawing materials; a chalkboard or large sheet of paper.

What to do

Gather the class together and discuss with them the different occasions when they have sent or received cards. Try to collect as many types of occasion as possible, and note them on a chalkboard or large sheet of paper. Show the children the selection of cards and encourage them to talk about some examples.

- *What occasion is the card for?*
- *Who is it for?*
- *What tells you this? Is it the picture? The words?*

Organise the class into groups of four. Explain that each group will have four cards, eight strips of paper and some crayons or marker pens. The task is to decide what occasion each card is designed for and to whom they would send it. They will record this information on the strips of paper. Model an example:

Good luck with your exam!	Brother

The intention is that the four children in each group will work together, all contributing to the discussion and the task, but each child will record for one card. Set a time limit of 15 minutes and monitor the groups' progress, helping when required.

Bring the class together again and ask each group to give a report on their work. Display their responses, as in Figure 6.

Explore with the children again the variety of occasions; the importance of the written messages on the front of and inside the card; the importance of the picture and its link to the message; and the appropriateness of all these to the recipient. Select one or two cards and check the children's understanding of how they work:

- *On what occasion would you send this card?*
- *Would you send it to your Mum? Your friend? Your brother?*
- *Why? Why not?*

Ask the children to think about an occasion in their family or school life which is coming up, and for which they would like to design and send a card. Explain that they can use the 'Planning a greetings card' sheet (photocopiable page 72) for this. Model the process on a chalkboard or large sheet of paper, filling in the details as suggested in Figure 7.

Further development

Encourage the children to make and develop their planned cards during choosing time or as part of their work programme. They will need additional art materials for this: coloured card, foil paper, glitter, glue sticks, scissors and so on.

THE WEATHER REPORT

Date: _____

Morning:

Afternoon:

Evening:

The general forecast for tomorrow is:

MY PERSONAL HOBBIES FACTFILE (1)

Name: _____

Age: _____

School: _____

Three favourite hobbies:

Hobby 1: _____

The first time I _____

_____

I wear _____

I need _____

I like _____ because _____

_____

The best part is _____

The worst part is _____

MY PERSONAL HOBBIES FACTFILE (2)

Hobby 2: _____

The first time I _____

_____

I wear _____

I need _____

I like _____ because _____

_____

The best part is _____

The worst part is _____

Hobby 3: _____

The first time I _____

_____

I wear _____

I need _____

I like _____ because _____

_____

The best part is _____

The worst part is _____

OCCASION CARDS

a bowling party	a disco
a visit to the cinema	football training
cycling in the forest	a country walk
swimming	a birthday party
a visit to the zoo	going on holiday
a visit to the beach	the gymnastics club
shopping in the town	

Scholastic
NON-FICTION WRITING
Workshop

NAME

IDEAL FOR...

drawing or design   description

price

FINDING THE FACTS

I want to know about

_____

When you have found a book about this,

1. Write down

- the title _____

- the author's name _____

- the publisher _____

---

2. Look at the contents page and note useful page numbers.

---

3. Look at the index and note useful page numbers.

---

4. Find the pages and look for the information you need.

5. Note down the information you find on scrap paper.

6. Complete the information sheet.

INFORMATION SHEET

Topic: _____

Fact 1:

Fact 2:

Fact 3:

Fact 4:

The book I used was:

Title _____

Author _____

Published by _____ Date _____

NAME

CALUM'S LETTER

30 Mayflower Road
Glasgow

Dear class,

    I fell off a high climbing frame. I had a swollen lip, a black eye and a bleeding nose. My dad took me to hospital and the doctors thought I had a broken nose but I didn't. I had to stay over night with my mum. The next day I went home with my mum, my dad and my sister they brought me a cake.

From calum

Scholastic
NON-FICTION WRITING
Workshop

DEAR CALUM

Dear Calum,

Thank you for your letter. I hope your head is better now. I am writing to tell you about something that happened to me.

The first thing that happened was _____

_____

_____

_____

Then _____

_____

_____

_____

and finally _____

_____

_____

_____

Love from

QUESTIONS ABOUT YOUR PRECIOUS OBJECT

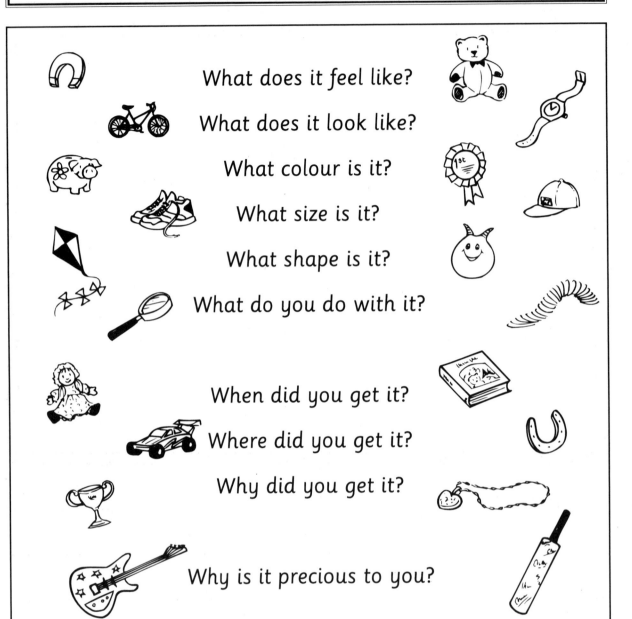

What does it feel like?

What does it look like?

What colour is it?

What size is it?

What shape is it?

What do you do with it?

When did you get it?

Where did you get it?

Why did you get it?

Why is it precious to you?

Scholastic
NON-FICTION WRITING
Workshop

MY PRECIOUS OBJECT

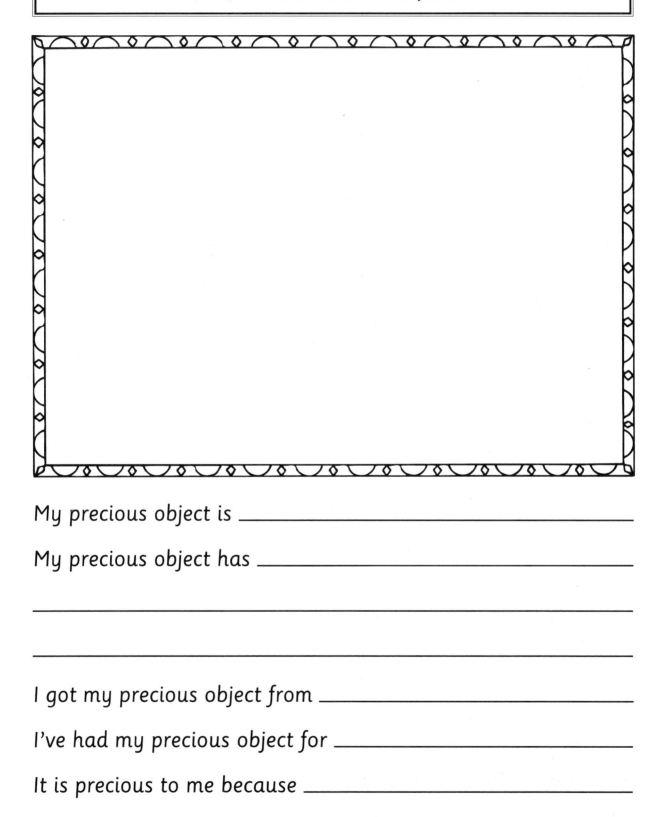

My precious object is _____

My precious object has _____

_____

_____

I got my precious object from _____

I've had my precious object for _____

It is precious to me because _____

_____

_____

WHAT I DID AT SCHOOL TODAY

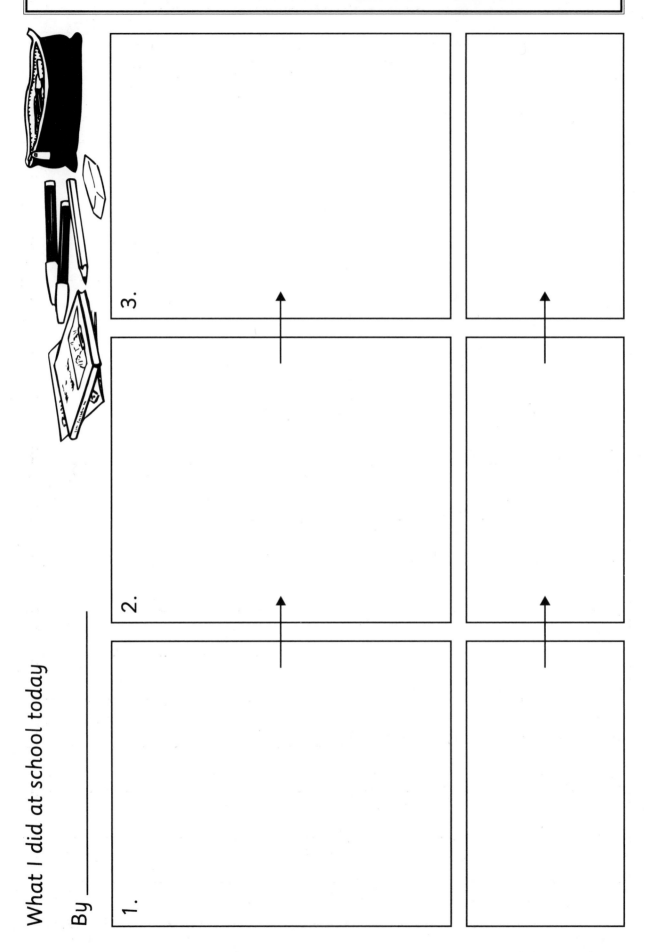

3.

2.

1.

What I did at school today

By _____

READ ALL ABOUT IT!

Baby Bear's Story

1.	
2.	
3.	
4.	

READ THE LABEL

Our
T-shirt

Our label

Our label tells you:

LABEL FOR A PAIR OF JEANS

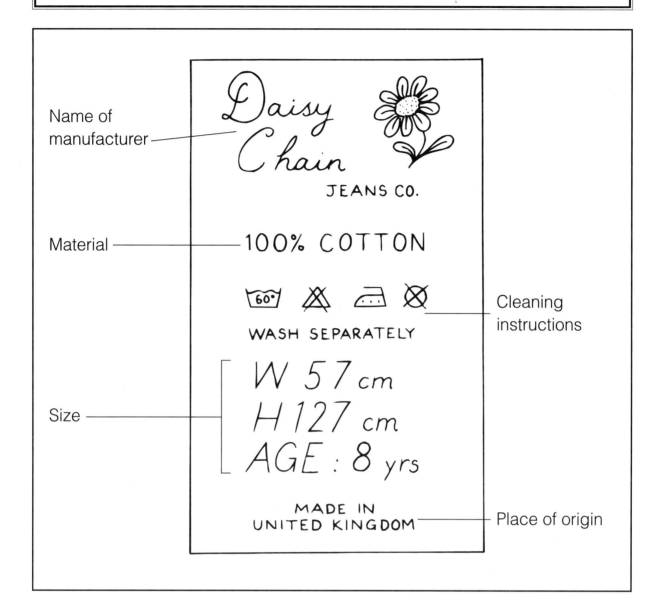

Name of manufacturer —— *Daisy Chain* JEANS CO.

Material —— 100% COTTON

Cleaning instructions

WASH SEPARATELY

Size —— W 57 cm
H 127 cm
AGE : 8 yrs

MADE IN
UNITED KINGDOM —— Place of origin

MY FAVOURITE SANDWICH

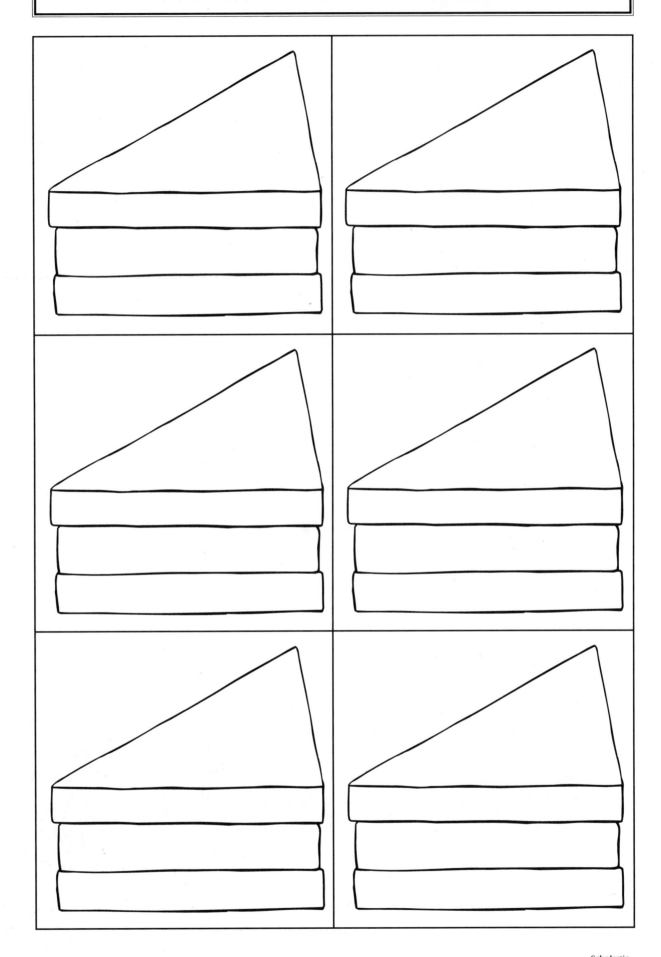

WHAT IS A GLOSSARY?

Match by drawing a line to the correct explanation

Climate

When land is covered with water.
This is usually caused by heavy rainfall.

Freezing

The view you can see all around you.

Landscape

The type and pattern of weather in a place or country.

Temperature

Very cold, a temperature at or below 0°C.

Flood

How hot or cold it is.

Rain

Electric flashes in the sky seen during thunderstorms.

CAN YOU EXPLAIN?

Why is the boy wearing a bandage?

Why is the dog wet?

Why is the girl's face covered in spots?

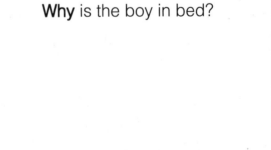

Why is the boy in bed?

WHAT'S IN THE LEAFLET?

Name of place: _____

Things to do:

Other information:

What makes it a good leaflet?

1. _____

_____

2. _____

_____

3. _____

_____

ALL ABOUT US

The book of our group

Contents

1

2

3

4

I CAN DO IT!

I can make a junk model.

I made a _____

This is how I did it.

First I

Next, I

Then I

Last of all, I

A NEWSDESK REPORT

Newsdesk report from _____

Date: _____ Time: _____

Place: _____

People: _____

What happened:

```
┌─────────────────────┐
│                     │
│                     │
│                     │
│                     │
│                     │
│                     │
│     (photograph)    │
│                     │
│                     │
│                     │
│                     │
│                     │
└─────────────────────┘
```

Scholastic
NON-FICTION WRITING
Workshop

CALENDAR

PLANNING A GREETING CARD

person _____

occasion _____

front picture and front message

inside message

Scholastic
WORKSHOP

Chapter Four

PERSUASION
AND DISCUSSION

INTRODUCTION

Persuasive writing is used to promote one particular point of view and to encourage others to see things in the same way. Discussion also presents viewpoints, but includes different or opposing arguments. Examples of persuasive writing are advertisements and posters persuading people to do or believe particular things. Examples of discussion occur when children try to agree on a way of doing something, or evaluate different ways of doing things. Discussion can be seen as a form of persuasive writing which offers alternative stances, giving reasons for each before recommending a conclusion.

Why persuasion and discussion matter

Both adults and children need to be able to recognise when something has been written to present only one point of view, and particularly when it is meant to persuade them to buy something, do something or behave in a certain way. This awareness is an important feature of a literate society.

As adults, we use persuasive and discussion writing when we make notes before going for a job interview, complaining in a shop or going to see the class teacher about an incident in school. In such cases, the need to convey information is limited to the need to influence the audience's viewpoint.

Young children do less of this type of writing than writing in the other non-fiction genres, but they are exposed to it in everyday life – when they watch adverts on TV or read them in comics; when they talk to other people to persuade them of a particular point of view; when they discuss what to spend their pocket money on. In school, when children are involved in planning campaigns to improve the quality of school meals or the use of the playground, they may be required to produce persuasive writing.

Experiencing 'persuasion and discussion' writing helps children to think clearly and critically, to listen and respond to others' opinions, to ask pertinent questions and to present an argument in a clear and coherent way. They not only learn to express their own viewpoints in persuasive ways, but become aware that facts can be interpreted in different ways and that a variety of opinions on an issue may be valid.

Children also need to learn that persuasion and discussion, though involving similar skills, can be opposite in terms of purpose. Persuasion is always one-sided, whereas discussion aims at reaching an 'objective' resolution in which different viewpoints are taken into account. For this reason, discussion is often problematic for younger children who have difficulty appreciating the viewpoints of others.

What children know about persuasion and discussion

As most parents know, the most powerful form of persuasion with which young children are familiar is the advert. Whether it occurs on hoardings, on packages, in comics or on television, the medium of the advertisement has a huge influence in persuading young children what to eat, wear, do, play with, watch, visit or listen to. Even before they start school, children may be able to identify brand names and written slogans from a logo or the context of a product.

Adults also often try to persuade individual children to do things: 'You really need to tidy your room. If you tidied your room, I'm sure you would find the Subbuteo figures that are missing. And then, if we cleared a space on the floor, we could play a game of Subbuteo.' All children will be familiar with the structure and language of verbal persuasion in the home setting. Similar examples occur in school, though these may contain less elaboration and may appear more like instructions, directions or requests. 'I think we should tidy the bricks up

now, because it's P2's turn to come to the playroom next. So come on, Saeed, you help Joanne to tidy the bricks away.' In some circumstances the persuasive language used may be subtle or even disguised.

Children are also aware of trying to persuade others to let them do or have something. They will often state their reasons: 'I really need to go to the newsagents. *Playdays* comes on Wednesdays and today is Wednesday. Please, please, please can we go?' It seems natural for them to 'state their position', 'make their point', sometimes 'elaborate on it' and sometimes 'reiterate', in speech. They do not always do this naturally in writing. However, it helps children's thinking and understanding of written forms and their real purposes to become more conscious of the strategies used in persuasion, and to persuade through writing as well as talk. Writing will also help them to organise their persuasive arguments in an effective way.

Children come across discussion in situations in which a decision has to be made, for example: 'Should I buy a ball or a book with my pocket money?' or 'What will we play at playtime today?' Within the curriculum, they are encouraged to enquire and make their own decisions about the best course of action – for example, in problem solving or during exploratory play. They may have to weigh up in their minds or in spoken language the advantages and disadvantages of a chosen action. For example, two children who are working together to build a model, following a plan, may decide to start at different points with different pieces of the kit – in which case, they will have to justify and discuss their choices and reach a decision together.

Discussions with young children tend to be presented orally, and few situations lend themselves to children reading a discussion. The most common experience of reading discussions occurs in stories, when characters have to make decisions or are offered alternatives. Even books for very young children may contain an element of decision-making which raises the opportunity to explore different perspectives and thus build an understanding of discussion. For example, in the book *Dear Zoo* by Rod Campbell (Picture Puffin, 1985), various animals are presented as potential pets and then dismissed as unsuitable for different but specific reasons. Discussions are often presented as following a fixed format:

- statement of the issue or proposal;
- arguments for;
- arguments against;
- final recommendation.

However, most young children do not adhere to this format in their oral or written work. They are more likely to raise points in an *ad hoc* way, as they think of them; and the sequence depends very much on the situation and who is involved.

KEY FEATURES

Discussion and persuasion have to be taught in contexts which are familiar and meaningful to the children. They need to be taught to recognise the very different purposes of, as well as the similarities and differences between, persuasion and discussion. For example, the question

'Should tigers live in zoos?' might be answered in a persuasive fashion by first stating the position of the speaker: 'Tigers shouldn't live in zoos because it is bad for them, it's not natural.' The speaker might then elaborate on the reasons why this is her/his own opinion: 'First, because they might be on their own and they will be lonely. Also, a cage is too small. Tigers need lots of space to run around.' Sometimes, the argument can include several different points: 'It is too cold here anyway. Tigers should live in hot countries like India or Pakistan.' Occasionally, a child will summarise at the end by reiterating her/his position in a different way: 'So I think there are lots of reasons for sending the tigers back and not bringing any more to our zoos.'

This same question would be dealt with quite differently through a discussion. The speaker might start with a recognition that there are two viewpoints: 'Well, some people think it is good to have tigers in zoos, so we can see them and learn about them and they are well looked after. Other people think it is cruel and unnatural.' They may elaborate on both viewpoints: 'There are not too many tigers left in the jungle, so it is good if zoos keep some to look after and maybe breed more. It is good to go to the zoo and see tigers – how they move, what they eat, what they look like. You can learn a lot, although some other people say it is cruel because tigers don't have enough space in the zoo to prowl and leap about. Also, usually there is only one or maybe two, and it would be better if there were more tigers together. Also, where tigers come from it is hot, not cold like here.' They may end by expressing

a personal view or making a particular recommendation: 'I think it is better for tigers to be left in the jungle, not to live in a zoo.'

Sometimes a discussion can be presented as two sides of an argument. This is how discussion often occurs in real life – for example:

Joanne 'Why can't we have a cat? Me and Calum would really like one, but you and Dad keep saying "No".'

Mum 'We can't have a cat because we live on a main road. And we live in a flat, so how can it go in and out? And Mum and Dad both work, so who is going to look after it?'

Joanne 'But Mansol has a cat and *she* lives on a busy road – she just lets it out the back. We could have a cat flap or just let it out when we're at home. Me and Calum will look after it, we promise. We could just have a house cat. So we *can* have a cat because it would be really friendly and cuddly and no work for you.'

Mum 'No, you *can't* have a cat, because of all the problems I've just explained.'

Although discussions like this will occur naturally, children need to be made aware of how they evolve and how they can help to clarify the arguments for and against.

In ***persuasion***, the speaker/writer:
• forms an opinion or position;
• gives reasons why he/she takes this position;
• summarises her/his conclusion.

In ***discussion***, the speaker/writer:
• recognises and states an issue;
• gives reasons why some people think one thing and some people think another;
• decides from the arguments what he/she thinks;
• summarises her/his conclusion or decision.

LEARNING DISCUSSION AND PERSUASION

In order to write persuasively, children need to learn that the purpose and audience for their writing must be clear. They should be encouraged to ask themselves and each other questions such as 'What am I trying to do?', 'Who am I trying to persuade?', 'What sort of arguments will capture this person's attention and persuade them?' and 'What is the best way to present the arguments and persuade this person?'

Children should understand that persuasive writing is often 'hard-hitting' and starts with an

opening statement which clearly and succinctly says what position or belief is being argued. The writer will then need to put the arguments in favour of her/his idea and to end with a summary and restatement of the basic position – 'So that's it and that's why.'

Persuasive advertising, in particular, has a positive emphasis or bias and is clearly directed at a particular type of person (for example, compare adverts for girls' and boys' toys). Adverts may also use attractive and eye-catching methods to grab the readers' interest and attention: written adverts are generally illustrated and have a short, snappy message in big clear print. The effect of persuasive writing is to draw readers in and make them identify with the message and images portrayed.

Linguistic features of written persuasion and discussion

Children need to know that these kinds of writing:
- are usually written in the present tense;
- make direct reference (at least in the examples the children will be dealing with) to the people/animals/things involved;
- use linking words such as 'because', 'therefore' and 'so';
- use words that address the reader directly;
- are often written from a personal standpoint ('I think').

For persuasive writing, children need to decide on and present the most important argument first and then link others to it. For discussion writing, children often need to present an argument and a counter-argument in sequence, then explain their own view.

How can persuasion and discussion be taught?

Teachers must find opportunities to develop this kind of talk and writing within natural contexts, so as to develop the children's understanding and skills. Such contexts occur both in play and in work across the curriculum, for example: predicting whether an object will float or sink and justifying that prediction to others; collaboratively planning a model of a boat which will float (discussing the alternatives, giving reasons and coming to conclusions); deciding collectively on the best route around the supermarket to collect the shopping on a list. Collaborative paired and group work, problem-solving activities and experiences of evaluating will all create opportunities for persuasion, discussion and argument.

Much of the work on this genre of writing will begin through talk with the teacher in class and group situations. When work progresses from talk to written recording, the teacher will act as a model and in many cases will record or scribe for the children. As with all written activities, the setting of audience and purpose will be important, as will the teaching of skills and key features (see above).

Organisation of this chapter

Because of the relationship between audience, purpose and context in these activities, it is difficult to organise the chapter into discrete sections. For this reason, the activities are grouped as follows:
- **Words** – I think, I believe, because, and so/therefore.
- **Structures** – stating a case or point of view, giving reasons for that viewpoint, giving an opposing viewpoint, reaching a conclusion based on the arguments.
- **Contexts** which bring key features together – making complex decisions, creating adverts, designing products.

Activity	Teaching content	Star rating	Group size	Photo-copiable
WORDS				
1 Bedtime in summer	Understanding other people's points of view. Using 'why' and 'because'.	✶	Ⓦ ⇨ 1	✓✓✓
2 Boxed in!	Stating a case and justifying an idea.	✶	Ⓦ ⇨ 2	✓✓
3 Save this tree	Persuading people to agree with us, using slogans and a petition.	✶✶✶	Ⓦ ⇨ 4 ⇨ Ⓦ	✓
4 Dark is good	Giving reasons for an unusual view.	✶✶✶	Ⓦ ⇨ 4	✓
5 Keep tigers in the jungle	Constructing opposite points of view, using slogans.	✶✶/✶✶✶	Ⓦ ⇨ 2 ⇨ Ⓦ	✓✓
6 Would you rather...?	Giving reasons for **not** doing something.	✶✶	Ⓦ ⇨ 1	✓✓✓
7 Help Little Red Riding Hood	Persuading a character in different ways.	✶/✶✶	Ⓦ ⇨ 1	
8 Read this book	Persuading people to read a book.	✶/✶✶✶	Ⓦ ⇨ 4 ⇨ 1	✓
STRUCTURES				
9 The missing pieces	Writing a letter of complaint.	✶✶	Ⓦ ⇨ 2	✓✓
10 Big? Bad? Who, me?	Putting the opposite case to a familiar view.	✶✶/✶✶✶	Ⓦ ⇨ 2	✓
11 Toenails	Features of a radio advertisement.	✶✶✶	Ⓦ ⇨ 2 ⇨ 6	✓✓✓
12 TV advert	Features of a TV advertisement.	✶✶	Ⓦ ⇨ 4	
CONTEXTS				
13 Free gift	Layout and design of a 'free gift' offer.	✶	Ⓦ ⇨ 4 ⇨ 2	
14 Where should we go?	Stating a case and giving reasons. Obtaining relevant information.	✶✶✶	Ⓦ ⇨ 4	✓
15 Good pet/bad pet	Reaching a conclusion after listing good and bad points.	✶/✶✶	Ⓦ ⇨ 4	✓
16 Special offer	Persuading someone to buy food using an advertisement sign.	✶/✶✶	Ⓦ ⇨ 2	✓✓
17 Bring and buy sale	Persuading someone to buy a second-hand toy using slogans.	✶	Ⓦ ⇨ 1	
18 Say you'll be there	Persuading a variety of people through a poster.	✶✶	Ⓦ ⇨ 2	✓✓
19 Oat Crispies or Rice Flakes	Designing a logo and package.	✶	Ⓦ ⇨ 2	✓
			Ⓦ = whole class	

BEDTIME IN SUMMER

Teaching content
Understanding other people's points of view.
Use of 'why' and 'because'.

What you need
The poem 'Bedtime in Summer' by Shirley
Hughes (printed on photocopiable page 97);
photocopiable page 98, writing materials; a
chalkboard or large sheet of paper.
Photocopiable page 99 could be used to extend
the activity.

What to do
It will be helpful if the class are already familiar
with the character Alfie, having listened to
some of Shirley Hughes' stories and had the
opportunity to read them for themselves.

Gather the class together to listen to the
poem 'Bedtime in Summer' by Shirley Hughes*.
Discuss how Alfie is feeling and why he wants
to stay up. List the children's ideas on the left-
hand side of a chalkboard or large sheet of
paper, under the heading 'Why stay up?
Because...'. Ask the children if they have ever
wanted to stay up late and for what reason. Add
their reasons to the list.

Now ask the children what they think Alfie
might say to his mum. List these suggestions in

the middle of the board or sheet, then examine
the wording to highlight key words which
might help persuade Mum. How will Alfie's
mother respond? Perhaps she has reasons for
thinking Alfie should stay upstairs and go to
sleep. Discuss her possible reactions and what
she might say. Write down key words and
phrases on the right of the board or sheet,
under the heading 'Why go to bed? Because...'.

Following this discussion, the children should
complete photocopiable page 98 by filling in
speech balloons for Alfie and Mum, based on
what they think will happen. Discuss these and
discover how many children think Alfie will stay
up and how many think he will go back to bed.

What do the children's own parents or
guardians think about bedtime in summer? Ask
the children to discuss this at home and bring
back to class reasons and opinions given by
parents or others. These reasons can be
discussed and added to the appropriate list.

Further development
Tell the children that you have heard about
Fairy Godmothers who sometimes grant special
wishes. Ask them to describe a wish they have.
It could be to have a pet, a special toy or a
computer game; or perhaps it's something they
want to do (such as learning how to ride a horse
or skate), or a place they want to visit; or
perhaps it's a different kind of wish entirely.
Ask the children to decide on a particular wish
and (working individually or in small groups)
to write a letter to persuade the Fairy Godmother
to make their wish come true. Appropriate
reasons must be given. Refer back to the
persuasive language highlighted during the
Alfie activity. Photocopiable page 99 could be
used to provide a writing frame for the letter.
* From *The Big Alfie and Annie Rose Storybook*
by Shirley Hughes (Red Fox, 1990).

BOXED IN!

Teaching content

Stating a case and justifying an idea.

What you need

Photocopiable pages 100 and 101, writing materials; a large sheet of paper labelled as in Figure 1.

What to do

The children should be familiar with the story of *Dear Zoo* by Rod Campbell (Picture Puffin, 1985). This story has a repetitive pattern of *I wrote to the Zoo to send me a ... They sent me a ... It was ... so I sent it back*, until the character is ultimately satisfied with a puppy. Each of the animals arrives in a different carrier – a box, a crate, a basket and so on. It would help to provide the book as a context and reminder. Focus the children's attention on photocopiable page 101. Ask them: *Is this the best way for the giraffe to travel?* Explain that there may be good reasons to move it in this way. Ask the children if they can think of any, and record their reasons in the first column of the large sheet of paper – for example:

• It's a tall box.
• The giraffe can look out the top.
• It can stand up inside it.
• It's the only box that the zoo has for giraffes!

Good reasons	Not that box	Better ideas

Figure 1

Now ask the children if they can think of any reasons why the giraffe should *not* go back in that box. Listen to their ideas and record them in the second column. They may suggest:

• It's cruel to keep it in a box.
• It can't move around or sit down.

Finally, ask the children if they could suggest a better way to send the giraffe back to the zoo. Arrange the children in pairs and give them time to discuss solutions. Hand out photocopiable page 100 and explain that you want them to draw a picture of the better way in the box provided and to write their reasons why below the picture. Some children may need to refer to the list already generated by the class, or may need you to provide additional words or scribe for them.

When the children have finished, select one or two completed sheets to show to the whole class. Collate the sheets in a class book entitled *Good Ways to Move a Giraffe*.

SAVE THIS TREE

Teaching content

Using words to get people to agree with us. Designing slogans for banners and badges, framing a petition.

What you need

Photocopiable page 102; art materials for making banners; sticky labels for badges; paper, pens; a copy of *Save This Tree* by Maggie Pearson (Hodder & Stoughton, 1991).

What to do

Give the children photocopiable page 102, which is an extract from *Save This Tree* by Maggie Pearson. Read out the text, then ask the children:

• What is happening?
• How do the children in the story feel?
• What could/should they do?

Note their ideas, then show them the front cover of the book (if you have it) to confirm or extend suggestions. Then say that the story characters have decided to hold a protest meeting on Saturday morning, to persuade people to support their view and save the tree. How could we help them?

Organise the class into four groups. Discuss the following with them:

1. *How to attract attention?* They will need more banners with slogans. *What to write on the banners?* One group designs and makes banners to take to the meeting.

2. *How to explain the problem and our viewpoint so as to get people to support us? What should we say to people?* One group lists suitable arguments with persuasive words and rehearses possible dialogue.

3. *What can we give people to wear?* One group designs and makes protest badges, using sticky labels.

4. *How can we record the number of people who are on our side?* A petition is needed. Work with this group to discuss what a petition is and to produce one for the 'Save This Tree' campaign. It should have a heading, a statement explaining the viewpoint and giving reasons for it, then space for lots of people to sign.

When groups have all prepared their material, the whole class can role-play the meeting, inviting the class next door to act as passers-by. Can they be persuaded to support the protest?

After the role play, take time to discuss the outcomes. *How successful were we in persuading people? What helped us – the banners? the badges? the petition?*

The children could also design a simple questionnaire to give to the other class after the 'meeting', asking questions such as:

• *What made you notice us?*
• *Which slogan did you like?*
• *How would you rate our badges?*
  (very good/OK/not very good)
• *Did you sign the petition?*
  (yes/no)

The responses to the questionnaires should be collated and discussed.

The children will probably want to know how the story ended, so (if possible) make the book available for them to read, or read it to them.

4

DARK IS GOOD

Teaching content

You can give reasons for believing the opposite of what someone else believes.

What you need

The extract from *The Owl Who Was Afraid of the Dark* by Jill Tomlinson printed below; sheets of newsprint, marker pens; photocopiable page 103, writing materials.

'...I want to go hunting with Daddy, but he always goes hunting in the dark, and I'm afraid of it.'

'How very odd,' said the old lady. 'Now, I love the dark. I expect you will when you are my age. DARK IS KIND.'

What to do

Explain to the children that Plop is a baby owl who is afraid of the dark. Each day, he meets someone who tells him good things about the dark. Today he has met an old woman who tells him that dark is kind. Ask the children to listen as you read the story extract aloud, then tell you why the old woman thinks dark is kind. She is trying to persuade Plop to believe this. Tell the children that other people in the story try to convince Plop that dark is exciting, fun, necessary, fascinating, wonderful and beautiful.

Organise the children into groups and explain to them that it is our job to persuade Plop that the dark is a good thing. Give out sheets of newsprint and copies of page 103. Ask each group to brainstorm all their ideas onto a sheet of newsprint. When each group has a list of ideas, they should decide on the three best arguments to make to Plop. These should be written onto photocopiable page 103. Each group should then present their case to the class.

If you were Plop, would you still be afraid of the dark?

'Tell me,' Plop said.

'Please,' said the old lady. 'Such a little word, but it works wonders.'

'Tell me, please,' said Plop obediently.

'Well, now,' the old lady began. 'Dark is kind in all sorts of ways. Dark hides things – like shabby furniture and the hole in the carpet. It hides my wrinkles and my gnarled old hands. I can forget that I'm old in the dark.'

'I don't think owls get wrinkles,' said Plop. 'Not Barn Owls, anyway. They just get a bit moth-eaten looking.'

'Don't interrupt!' said the old lady. 'It is very rude to interrupt. Where was I? Yes – dark is kind when you are old. I can sit in the dark and remember. I remember my dear husband, and my children when they were small, and all the good times we had together. I am never lonely in the dark.'

'I haven't much to remember, yet,' said Plop. 'I'm rather new, you see.'

'Dark is quiet, too,' said the old lady, looking hard at Plop. 'Dark is restful – unlike a little owl I know.'

'Me?' said Plop.

'You,' said the old lady. 'When I was a little girl, children were seen but not heard.'

'I'm not children,' said Plop. 'I'm a Barn Owl.'

'Same thing,' said the old lady. 'You remind me very much of my son.'

from *The Owl Who Was Afraid of the Dark* by Jill Tomlinson (Mammoth, 1992)

5

KEEP TIGERS IN THE JUNGLE

***** ✷✷✷✷ ⓦ→ⅱ→ⓦ ⟨40⟩

Teaching content

Different people may have different views on an issue. Short, snappy slogans are required for banners and signs.

What you need

Photocopiable pages 104* and 105, writing materials; a chalkboard or large sheet of paper.

What to do

Gather the class together and tell them that today they will be looking at two sides of an argument before they decide which one they agree with. Hand out photocopiable page 104 (one between two) and discuss what the people are protesting about. What is their viewpoint? What reasons are they giving for leaving tigers in the jungle? Examine the details of the wording on the banner and signs. Note key phrases on a chalkboard or large sheet of paper.

Ask the children to think about what is being said, and to consider whether they might support the protest. Do not take any feedback at this point. Tell the children that before they decide,

they should ask themselves 'Is there another point of view?' Will tigers be better off in the jungle? For example, tigers in the jungle may not be protected from hunters, or the jungle may be destroyed by farmers. Take some feedback on this.

Now give out copies of photocopiable page 105 and explain that the children should work in pairs to show a demonstration for the opposing view. Show them how to put the sheets side by side, and ask them to fill in the blanks on the banner and signs. This can be done by examining the wording and writing 'opposite' statements (or finding an 'opposite' rhetorical phrase.

When the pairs have completed the sheet, ask for examples and list these on the chalkboard or large sheet of paper beside their 'opposites'.

Now ask the children to think about the pro-zoo arguments. Do they agree with this view? Has anyone changed their opinion?

The activity can end with a vote for or against 'Keeping Tigers in the Jungle', and a conclusion: 'We think that ...'

Further development
For older children, this activity would be a good subject for a written discussion in recount mode. They could be asked to write an account of the activity, stating the problem, putting forward each argument in turn, then describing the voting and the result.
* (This sheet is based on an illustration in *Tiger and Me* by Kaye Umansky, illustrated by Suzi Jenkin-Pearce, Red Fox, 1991.)

6
WOULD YOU RATHER...?

Teaching content
To persuade someone *not* to do something they want to do, you have to make a good case.

What you need
Photocopiable page 106 (taken from *Would You Rather?* by John Burningham, Collins Picture Lions, 1984); photocopiable page 107, writing materials. Photocopiable page 108, taken from *Chips and Jessie* by Shirley Hughes (Harper Collins, 1985), could be used in a follow-up activity (see 'Further development').

What to do
Gather the class together and examine photocopiable page 106, which is an extract from the John Burningham book *Would You Rather?* Ask the children to say which they would rather have happen and why. Listen to about six to eight of their ideas, then ask them how the child in the book would feel if her/his dad did a dance at school or her/his mum had a row in a café? Elicit the response 'embarrassed'. What other embarrassing things might the parents in the story do? Explore why these things would cause embarrassment.

Move on to consider how the parents in the book might be persuaded not to do something, or at least not to do it again. Model this using

one of the two examples: If the dad was going to do a dance at school, how could the child persuade him not to?

- *He looks very silly when he's dancing.*
- *All my friends would laugh at him.*
- *He might injure his back and not be able to play badminton.*
- *People might not take him seriously if he did a silly dance and made a fool of himself.*

Try to elicit three good reasons from the children. Now ask them how we should let the dad know. Encourage the children to suggest writing a letter, because if it is written down maybe he won't forget. Explain the 'Please don't' writing frame (photocopiable page 107) and use it to model the letter for 'a child's dad did a dance at school'. (Maintain the fictional context for this.)

The children should now invent another embarrassing incident and write their own letter to the parent in the book, asking her/him not to do it and giving their reasons. If you prefer, the children could work as a group on this task. The completed letters could be signed and 'posted' on a noticeboard.

Further development
As a follow-up activity, the children could use photocopiable page 108 as a stimulus for role play involving children making unreasonable (or perhaps quite reasonable) requests and parents refusing.

7
HELP LITTLE RED RIDING HOOD
*** W→✝ ⟨30⟩

Teaching content
Persuading a character in different ways and giving reasons.

What you need
One sheet of A4 card per child, marker pens; rulers, wooden sticks or rolls of paper; a prepared sign on card (see below).

What to do
This activity combines drama and writing. You may wish to organise space in the classroom for all the children to move around and act out their scenarios, or use different rooms for drama and writing.

Start the activity by setting the context: the story of Little Red Riding Hood. Play out the scenarios of packing the basket, saying goodbye to her mother and beginning to walk through the woods. Remind the children about the Big Bad Wolf, who could be in the woods, behind a tree or in Grandma's house.

Now divide the class into two groups. For the next part, one group will be Little Red Riding Hoods walking through the woods. The children in the other group are each going to stop a Little Red Riding Hood and warn her. What will they say? Give the 'warning' group a little time to think, then act out the scenario. At an appropriate point, stop the children and ask: *What is the warning?* Suggestions may include:

- *Don't go any further.*
- *Don't talk to strange wolves.*
- *Danger ahead!*
- *Don't go off the path.*

Gather the children together and ask them why they should warn her. Again, take suggestions, prompting if necessary.

- *It's dangerous there.*
- *It's not safe.*
- *The wolf might catch her.*
- *She shouldn't be on her own.*

Now tell the children that they are going to try to persuade Little Red Riding Hood to turn round. What could they say to her?

- *Go back!*
- *Stay on the path.*
- *You're safer at home.*
- *Your Mum might be worried.*

This time, choose the other group to be Little Red Riding Hood. When you say 'Stop', the members of the first group each have to find a Little Red Riding Hood and give her a positive message to persuade her to go back home.

For the last part of the session, return to the classroom and hand out one piece of A4 card to each child. Tell the children that they are now going to make a sign to use the next time they enact the scenario. Show the children the card sign you have made previously. Model this by showing them that on one side you have written a warning message in big letters. When you turn the banner round, the other side has a positive message to persuade Little Red Riding Hood to go back and keep safe.

The children will need to attach rolled paper, a ruler or a wooden stick to the sign to hold it up. When these have been completed, use them in a final version (or in further versions) of the drama scenario.

8

READ THIS BOOK

Teaching content

Persuading people to read a book and giving reasons for doing so.

What you need

A child's favourite book (from home or from the class/school library); your own favourite children's book; a large sheet of paper or chalkboard; photocopiable page 109, writing materials.

What to do

Two days before this activity, ask the children to choose one of their favourite books (either from home or from the school) and think about why they like it. They may appreciate the pictures, the print, the layout, the story/content or even some use of the book (for example, having the story read to them before going to sleep). Tell them to bring this book to school

(with permission, if necessary) to share with a small group in the class.

On the day, start by modelling the activity yourself. You will, of course, have to select a book at the children's level, since the purpose of the activity is to persuade the children to read it. It would thus be helpful to choose a book that the children have not seen before. Show them the book and, using the phrase 'You should read this book because...', give the children your reasons.

Now explain to the class that they are going to work in groups of four. Each child in turn will show the others her/his selected book and give reasons for reading it. Encourage the children to talk about their books in such a way that the others will really want to read it: make it sound exciting or scary, be enthusiastic about it, point to good illustrations and so on.

Give the children time to carry this out in their groups. Then ask the class what would make them want to read someone else's choice of book. Were they persuaded by anyone in their group? If so, what did he/she do or say to persuade them? Record some of these reasons on a chalkboard or large sheet of paper.

Finally, give a copy of photocopiable page 109 to each child and ask them to write down three good reasons which would persuade others to read their book. Their reasons could be shared at a Together Time, or could be collated in a class book of *Books Worth Reading*.

STRUCTURES

9

THE MISSING PIECES

[**] (W)→ (40)

Teaching content

Awareness of audience and purpose when making a complaint. The format of a letter.

What you need

A new jigsaw (at an appropriate level of difficulty) from which four pieces have been removed (see below); photocopiable pages 110 and 111, writing materials; a chalkboard or large sheet of paper.

What to do

Remove the four pieces at the bottom right-hand corner from a new jigsaw. Put these pieces aside to enclose with the reply to the class letters of complaint.

Introduce the new jigsaw at a choosing time, and await the reaction of the children who use it. When they explain the problem at report-back time, ask the class to suggest a possible course of action. Discuss the possibility of complaining – *Who to? How can we contact them?* Encourage the children to examine the jigsaw box for relevant information. If necessary (and appropriate), find out where the jigsaw was purchased or ordered from. Alternatively, attach a fictitious name and address label.

Discuss with the class the advantages and disadvantages of different ways of complaining – face to face, on the telephone and in a letter. Make sure that the circumstances require a letter. Ask the children to consider what the content of this should be.

• First, specify the complaint. What is the best wording for this?

• Next, consider how to make your feelings about the problem known.

• Now suggest how the situation could be put right.

• Finally, consider the best way of ending the letter.

Note the children's suggestions on a chalkboard or large sheet of paper, then ask them what more will be required to make a letter. Introduce photocopiable page 110, which is a letter frame with the jigsaw company's name, the date and so on. Discuss who will receive the letter and how he/she should be addressed. If modelling is necessary at this stage, ask the children to help you create a large-scale master copy of the letter; otherwise, ask the children to work in pairs or groups (of up to four) to create their own drafts using photocopiable page 110. Examine these and choose the best one, or select good features for a 'composite' fair copy version.

Say that you will ask the school secretary to post the letter. Allow a suitable interval, then arrange for a reply to arrive (with an appropriate postmark) enclosing the missing pieces.

MANAGER

Photocopiable page 111 can be used for this purpose. Read the reply to the class and discuss its content and wording. *How does it compare with our letter? Can we tell how the writer feels about the situation? Should we now reply with a letter of thanks?*

10

BIG? BAD? WHO, ME?

Teaching content

Putting the opposite case to a familiar view, using a story character to state his own viewpoint.

What you need

A large sheet of paper, marker pens; masks or puppets (optional); copies of photocopiable page 112 cut in half, pens or pencils, scissors, adhesive.

What to do

The children will be familiar with the story of Little Red Riding Hood, and with wolf stories from other books such as *Revolting Rhymes* by Roald Dahl (Picture Puffin, 1984) and *Clever Polly and the Stupid Wolf* by Catherine Storr (Young Puffin, 1967). The context for this activity is an interview with the Big Bad Wolf, to let him put forward the case that, in fact, he has been misinterpreted and is not evil at all. This activity lends itself to role play before the children start to write. (You may wish to use puppets or masks.)

Start by recalling the bad things that the Wolf did in the story. Record some of these on a large sheet of paper.

The story says:

Big. Bad.

Frightened Red Riding Hood.

Pushed Grandma into a cupboard.

Pretended to be someone else.

Now explain to the children that they are going to work in pairs. One child will be a television interviewer, and the other will be the Wolf. The first child should ask 'Are you a Big Bad Wolf?' and the other child, in role, should give a reply explaining why he is not really bad. To help the children, model the interview with yourself in the role of the Wolf. Let the children ask you questions, and offer replies:

Q Are you the Big Bad Wolf?

A But I'm a kind, gentle creature. Everyone loves me. You can see by my friendly smile...

Q Didn't you frighten Little Red Riding Hood?

A I wouldn't hurt a fly.

Q Did you disguise yourself as Little Red Riding Hood's Granny?

A I would never pretend to be someone else.

Q Did you lock Granny in the cupboard?

A Who, me? You've got it all wrong...

Encourage the children to think of more questions and answers. Then allow enough time for both children in each pair to take turns at being the Wolf and the interviewer. Give each child half a copy of photocopiable page 112, and tell them to write down in the speech bubble what the Big Bad Wolf might say to state his case. They should then cut out the speech bubbles to add to a frieze showing the Wolf on television (see Figure 2).

Figure 2

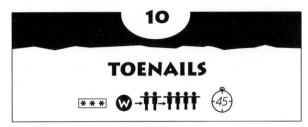

TOENAILS

Teaching content

A radio advert is different from a TV advert, since the former has no visual content. Language is thus the key feature. The language and structure have to be clear and precise.

What you need

An enlarged copy of photocopiable page 113, displayed on a chalkboard, card or OHT; a list of products cut from photocopiable page 114, shaken up and presented in a box or hat; photocopiable page 115, writing materials.

What to do

Display an enlarged copy of page 113, showing the poem 'Toenails' by Michael Rosen*. Read the poem aloud to the children. Explore with them what the writer is trying to get you to do. How does he try to persuade you to grow toenails? (Some children may also realise that the author is making fun of advertisements – but for the purposes of this activity, take his 'message' at face value.) Go through each part of the poem, asking the children to identify the strategies being used to persuade. List these on the chalkboard:

• stating that lots of people do or have something;

• stating its good points quickly and directly;
• getting one person to say how good it is;
• concluding by telling you to do the same as that person.

Ask the children to describe other adverts that they might have heard on the radio – for example, for toothpaste, shampoo, cat food. (If necessary, play them some adverts on a local radio station, or use ones you have taped from the radio.) Select one of these, such as Catto Cat Food, and involve the children in modelling an example in the format of photocopiable page 113. The model advert can be written on a chalkboard or a large sheet of paper:

More and more people in Britain today
are using
Catto.
Tasty and easy to open,
Catto contains all the things that cats enjoy
and need to keep healthy.
We spoke to Daphne Perks of Great Yarmouth.
'Yes, my cats love being fed on **Catto**.
I've got lots of flavours of **Catto**.
Rabbit ones for Ginger
and fishy ones for Fluffy.
They're brilliant.'
Be like Daphne.
Keep your cat happy.
Get **Catto**.

Pair the children up and explain the photocopiable sheet 'A radio advert for ...' (page 115). Now each pair can write an advert based on Michael Rosen's poem using page 115 as a frame. To make it more interesting, give them a 'product' to advertise. Each pair pick a product slip from the hat or box and work together to write the advert. Round this off with each pair joining three more pairs to perform their adverts to one another.

Written adverts can be displayed on the wall or in a book, with the question *Which would you choose?*

* From *The Hypnotiser* by Michael Rosen, illustrated by Martin Chatterton (Harper Collins, 1990).

12

TV ADVERT

Teaching content

TV adverts use images, characters, stories and music to persuade viewers to buy certain products.

What you need

A variety of product packs (for example: yoghurt, ice cream, fish fingers, sweets, chocolates); sheets of newsprint, marker pens; a chalkboard or large sheet of paper.

What to do

Gather the class together and ask them to name their favourite TV adverts. Tell them about your own favourite. List on the chalkboard five or six of the most popular, including your own. Explore with the children the reasons for the choices: music, imagery, humour and so on. Organise the children into five or six mixed-ability groups, giving each group a large sheet of newsprint and a marker pen. Allocate one of the listed adverts to each group, and put the product name at the top of their sheet.

Explain to the children that they have to give reasons why they like this advert. Nominate a scribe for each group, who will write or draw the reasons. Tell the children that it is their ideas you want, and you are not too worried about spelling.

After 15 minutes, gather the class around you to look at similarities and differences between their ideas. Make sure that everyone agrees on the key points:

* pictures (images);
* colours;
* characters;
* storyline;
* tune or jingle;
* excitement or humour;

* being about something we like.

If necessary, introduce the children to the word 'jingle'.

Stress to the children that they have listed the important general features of a TV advert. Explore the question of why manufacturers put adverts on TV. What does your favourite advert make you want to do? Elicit the response that adverts are designed to make you buy something or do something. Emphasise that TV adverts are one way of persuading people to do something or buy something, and point out that simply enjoying the advert may be enough to make people remember and choose a product.

Let the children return to their working groups. Give a distinctive product box, carton or packet to each group, telling them that their task is to make up a short TV advert for that product. Tell them that they should consider:

* music and jingles;
* actions;
* words.

The children may need your help in developing their ideas. When they have finished the task, they should perform their advert for the other groups, who can evaluate it using the key points as criteria.

Further development

A cassette recording, or even a videotape, of the groups' adverts could be made and evaluated by the class.

13

FREE GIFT

Teaching content

To attract attention, the following are effective: big, bold print, a clear message and a picture.

What you need

Cereal boxes with 'free gift' offers printed on them, a small collection of commercial 'free gifts' (such as cereal-box toys, football stickers, pencil tops); paper, marker pens.

What to do

Show the children your collection of 'free gift' items and ask them if they know what all these have in common. If necessary, lead them to the answer through discussion and questioning. The children will recognise that the items are all 'free gifts' available with purchased products.

Ask the children about their experiences of 'free gifts':

- *What did you get?*
- *Where did you get it?*
- *Did it come as a surprise?*
- *Did you know there was a free offer?*
- *How did you know?*

This will lead the children to discuss adverts on TV announcing 'free offers', leaflets or posters advertising 'free offers' and packaging labelled 'Free Offer' or 'Gift'. Organise the class into groups, giving each group two or three appropriate cereal boxes. Can they find the writing which says 'Free Gift' or 'Offer', and a picture of the gift or offer? Having identified these, they should cut them out.

Ask each group to examine their cut-outs to find three things which helped them to 'see' the free offer clearly. Their reporting back on this should point to such features as:

- big writing;
- clear writing;
- bright colours;
- fancy borders;
- exclamation marks;
- clear pictures;
- bright pictures.

Explain to the children that these features, as well as the 'free gift' itself, help to attract people and persuade them to buy the product. How often have they seen a box with a 'free offer' on it and asked a parent to buy it?

Pair the children up. Explain that each pair is going to decide on a 'free gift' and design the text and picture to attract people to it. They may choose one of the 'free gifts' provided, or invent one of their own.

The finished drawings and writing should be mounted and displayed with a caption: *Which free gift would you choose?*

Children may wish to repeat this activity with other products, such as comics or games.

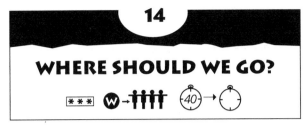

WHERE SHOULD WE GO?

Teaching content

Awareness of the purpose and audience of a brochure. Writing questions to obtain relevant information. The structure of a letter and layout of a brochure.

What you need

Addresses of several possible destinations for a school trip; a chalkboard or large sheet of paper; photocopiable page 116, writing materials; writing paper, envelopes.

What to do

This activity will require several sessions of 30 to 40 minutes. It should take place shortly before a school trip or outing. Remind the class that the time for their school trip is approaching, and ask them to suggest some good places not too far from the school. (You may suggest ideas if the children show little knowledge.) If possible, the destinations should be linked to current or recent projects. Make a list of suggestions (names only).

Ask the children to work in groups of four to six. Each group should choose a possible location (for example: a country farm because we are studying weather, growth and animals;

a castle because we are studying life in the Middle Ages; a mosque because we are studying great religions of the world). The group task is to write to the location staff, giving details of the class's requirements and asking for information about the location. Discuss the content of letters with the children. What information should we provide for the person who will receive our letter? It is necessary to explain who we are, why we are interested, when we might want to visit. Record their ideas on a chalkboard or large sheet of paper, under the heading 'What to tell'. Move on to discuss 'What information do we require?' List these ideas under the heading 'What to ask' – for example, *Do you have ...? Is there ...? How much will it cost?* Finally, discuss 'How to finish' and list some possibilities suggested by the children.

Give each group a copy of photocopiable page 116 to work out their first draft. Discuss the drafts, then remind the children of the correct format and layout for a letter (sender's address, date, directed to, salutation and so on). Help them to prepare fair copies for (actual) posting.

While the children await replies, the class should discuss criteria for selecting a destination. When these are agreed, they should be 'published' (listed and added to the wall display). When the replies arrive, the groups can examine and review the brochures, leaflets and so on. Have their questions been answered? Does the destination satisfy the criteria agreed upon?

Now the remit for each group is to persuade the others that theirs is the best destination. Each group should prepare a two-minute presentation in which to give their reasons. After the presentations, the children vote and a destination is chosen.

Further development

Follow-up might include writing again to the chosen destination to make a booking.

Note: If you want to carry out this activity but cannot afford a major outing, find some easy destinations within walking distance of the school such as a shop, a garden centre or a local hairdressing salon. Alternatively, set the activity in an imaginary context, using a known story character such as Paddington Bear. The children can help him choose and plan his day out. Paddington might enjoy visiting his relatives in the forests of Peru: booking a plane, taking presents with him, planning his flight and overland route on a world atlas, obtaining a new passport and a Spanish phrasebook...

15

GOOD PET/BAD PET

*** W→ 𝗍𝗍𝗍𝗍 (45)

Teaching content

You have to look at good points and bad points before making a decision.

What you need

A copy of *Dear Zoo* by Rod Campbell (Picture Puffin, 1984) or pictures of animals including a frog, a giraffe, a lion, a snake, a monkey, a camel and a puppy; photocopiable page 117, writing materials; an enlarged version of page 117 on a chalkboard or large sheet of paper.

What to do

Read the book *Dear Zoo* to the children. Make the point that the child decided on the puppy because he was 'just right'. All the other animals had something 'wrong' that the child did not like. Recall each animal and the criticism raised.

Alternatively, if you do not have access to the book, use pictures of animals (see above) to tell a story about a child who wanted a pet and asked the zoo to send him one. The zoo sent six animals in succession, starting with a lion and following with a giraffe, a camel, a frog, a snake and a monkey. Each of these animals had some drawback as a pet. The children should suggest what the problems might have been, for example:

- lion – too fierce;
- giraffe – too tall;
- camel – too grumpy;
- frog – too jumpy;
- snake – too scary;
- monkey – too naughty.

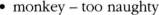

Eventually the zoo sent a puppy. The puppy was just right.

Model use of the pet evaluation sheet (photocopiable page 117) on a chalkboard or large sheet of paper:

Pet's name: frog

Good points	Bad points
	too jumpy

Ask the children if they can suggest any other bad points about the frog to extend the list. Can they suggest any good points? List these.

Decide with the children whether this would be a good pet or a bad pet to have. Would they recommend getting one? Model the final part of the pet evaluation sheet showing the children how to select the appropriate choice by deleting the inappropriate one:

> So I would say this would make a good/bad pet.
>
> Do/Don't get it.

Give each group one of the other 'not right' animals (monkey, lion, giraffe, camel, snake) and copies or one copy of the pet evaluation sheet. Ask them to complete it as you did for the frog. Emphasise that they should list all the reasons for and against, and try to weigh these before coming to a conclusion. The group can work together on the evaluation sheet, or each child can fill in an individual sheet.

The completed evaluation sheets could be made into a book and put in the class or school library, with the caption:

> Thinking of buying a pet? Read this first!

16

SPECIAL OFFER

Teaching content

Advertisements are designed to persuade people to buy products by providing an attractive image and simple text.

What you need

A selection of food adverts from magazines or leaflets; photocopiable page 118, writing materials; collage and art materials; photocopiable page 119.

What to do

As preparation for this activity, the children should recently have experienced sandwich making. Ask them to look out for adverts and special offer signs in their local shops or supermarket, as well as in magazines. What was the 'eye-catch' in each case? Discuss their feedback briefly, and create a small display of examples.

Tell the children that they will work in pairs to design an advert for a 'super sandwich', which can be sold in a class sandwich shop or the school cafeteria. First, each pair must decide on the super sandwich. What kind of bread?

MEGABITE

sardines, cheese, olives, peanut butter, salad and Marmite

Enjoy!

What kind of filling? The children should discuss with their partners and note ideas in visual and written form on photocopiable page 118. Some ideas can be shared briefly.

Now ask the pairs to consider how they will design the advert. Encourage them to analyse the adverts in the display as well as what they remember from shops. List appropriate criteria for an advert under the headings 'picture' (bright, colourful, attractive) and 'words' (clear, funny, easy to read). Ask the children: is the price important? Refer back to the sample material to look for examples such as 'Two for the price of one' or 'Special offer', and discuss the meanings of such phrases.

The pairs now work on developing a picture and wording for their super sandwich advert. This could be a very simple drawing activity for younger children, or a more complex and long-term project for older pupils (for example, they might want to make a sandwich and photograph it, or to use cut-and-stick lettering which takes time to produce). Decide how much time is available, and help children to set targets.

When the adverts are finished, they should be displayed and discussed. Does each one meet the agreed criteria? Which seem particularly successful? Which would persuade us to buy the sandwich? Why? Photocopiable page 119 can be given to each pair for them to evaluate another pair's advert.

17

BRING AND BUY SALE

Teaching content

Using slogans to persuade someone to buy a second-hand toy.

What you need

Children's used toys from home; A3 sheets of card or coloured paper; white paper cut in circles, rectangles and squares for labelling, glue, felt-tipped pens.

What to do

The context for this activity could be a bring and buy sale, a Christmas fair, a charity event or a play situation in which children have the opportunity to persuade others to buy something. A few days before the event, ask the children to bring a toy to school which they no longer use or play with. Explain that someone else may now wish to buy it, and that they should think of what they enjoyed about it that might persuade other children or parents to buy it now. The children will, of course, have to ask permission from home.

Arrange for these toys to be brought in on the day before the bring and buy sale (or similar event). Gather the class together and select one child to bring out her/his toy and explain why it would be a good toy to buy. He/she might say:
- it's a friendly teddy;
- it's cuddly;
- it would be good for a little sister/brother;
- there are clothes to put on it.

Repeat this with some other children, to encourage the children to state their reasons orally. Now explain that we have to find an effective way to display the toys so that people can see them clearly and read the reasons for buying them.

Model the display with an example given to you by one of the children. Position the toy in the middle of a sheet of card or coloured paper, and show the children four circular pieces of paper which will be stuck on to surround it. Explain that they have to write a different reason on each circle to persuade people to buy the toy. (See Figure 3.)

You may have to scribe or provide words for some children, depending on their ability; and you may wish to work on this with a smaller group while the other children are involved in different activities.

The toys and cards should be displayed on the day of the sale, with tags showing appropriate

Figure 3

prices. Try to make time for the children to look at each display board and to decide which toy they would be persuaded to buy and for what reasons.

This activity also links well with the project 'Our Good Toy Guide' in the Key Stage 1 *Non-Fiction Writing Projects* book.

18

SAY YOU'LL BE THERE

✱✱ ⓦ→👥 ⑥⓪

Teaching content
Persuading a variety of people through a poster. Key features of an effective poster – title, content, layout.

What you need
Sheets of A3 paper, strips of card for labels, pre-cut pictures or photos of teddy bears, felt-tipped pens; photocopiable pages 120 (enlarged) and 121, writing materials.

What to do
Gather the class together and set the context for this activity by explaining that they are going to help you make a poster to persuade children and adults to come to a Teddy Bears' Picnic. The activity could be linked to an actual picnic which will take place, or to a theme or story.

Show the children the 'Great day out' poster (an enlarged copy of page 120) and ask them what in the picture would persuade them to want to go there. They may suggest:

- There's lots to do there.
- It tells you clearly what there is.
- The pictures are exciting.
- It tells you how to get there.

Take the blank sheet of A3 paper and begin to model the design of a new poster by asking *What will the title be?* The children may suggest:

- **Come to the Teddy Bears' Picnic!**
- **Everyone welcome at the Teddy Bears' Picnic!**
- **Don't miss the Teddy Bears' Picnic!**
- **Teddy Bears' Picnic – One Day ONLY!**

As the children offer suggestions, draw their attention to the kind of language being used to persuade: don't miss, come to, everyone welcome and so on. Now decide where this title should go, and add it to your poster.

Next, discuss the key events. What would attract you to come to a Teddy Bears' Picnic? Again, offer ideas and take children's suggestions:

- Free honey sandwiches.
- Games to play.
- Prizes and competitions.
- Free entry.

Record a few of these on strips of card to add to your poster. Show the children the teddy bear pictures and ask them to decide how many should be used and where they should go. Discuss the importance of having a clear

layout, so that the poster is easy to follow and not too cluttered.

Finally, ask the children: *What else could be added to persuade parents and grandparents to come too?* They may suggest:

- Free parking.
- A map showing how to get there.
- A play area for babies.

Add these in appropriate places on the poster. Review what you have done so far to create an effective poster. You have thought of:

- a bright and persuasive title;
- suitable words to attract people to come;
- the overall layout of the poster.

Depending on the age of the children, you may wish to end the activity at this point and implement the follow-up the next day. The children should then work in pairs to create their own poster from a choice of topics, depending on your class themes or seasonal events (for example: Fireworks Display, Christmas Illuminations, Family Fun Day, Easter Parade). Encourage them to use the poster to advertise the best features of the event. Photocopiable page 121 should be given to the children to help them at the drafting stage.

Further development

The children could display their posters and write a letter to another class inviting them to visit and judge which poster would persuade them to come to an event and why.

19

OAT CRISPIES OR RICE FLAKES

Teaching content

Product packaging is designed to attract the attention of potential buyers. Designers achieve this through their use of colour and pattern, words, print style and images.

What you need

The fronts of various cereal boxes; photocopiable page 122, also an enlarged version; paper, card, pencils, marker pens.

What to do

Divide the class into groups and give each group a variety of cereal box fronts. Explain that everyone is going to join in a game in which you will call out the name of a particular breakfast cereal. The group that has the product whose name you call out stand up. The class help to check that the children standing have matched correctly.

When all the examples have been called, explore with the children how they knew which was which. Some will say they read the name. Explore this by looking at print style, size, shape and colour. Others will say 'It always has the same picture/character.' Explore this by looking at choice of picture/symbol, attractiveness, colours.

Is there anything else on the packet fronts which might be important? Ask the children to look at the sample box fronts and to feedback ideas (such as a special offer or reduced price, a free gift or a competition).

Explain that someone (a designer) has planned the box or package in a special way to persuade people to buy the product. Tell the children that they are now going to have the opportunity to be designers. Use an enlarged version of the 'Design brief' sheet (photocopiable page 122) and model how to complete it using a particular brand of cereal. Remind the children about wording, print size and style, colours, pattern, pictures/characters and special features.

Now ask the children to work in pairs, creating the box design for a new kind of cereal (on the 'Design brief' sheet). They can call this product either Oat Crispies or Rice Flakes, then decide:
- how the name will be printed;
- what the picture will show;
- how these will fit together on the box front.

When the children have completed the task, ask each pair to introduce their ideas and display their sheet. Discuss with the class which designs are most effective and which product they would buy. Should the name of the manufacturer and a 'special offer' be added?

Further development

Ask the children to look at supermarket displays and note which cereal boxes are the most noticeable and attractive. In the classroom, make a display of cereal box fronts with comment cards (*I like this because...* or *I don't like this because...*).

BEDTIME IN SUMMER

Lying in bed,
not a bit sleepy,
listening to lots of things
going on outside.
People chatting,
and watering their gardens,
and mowing the grass.
Birds calling,
boys shouting,
music from open windows
and a smell of supper.
The sun's still up.
It's slanting in under the curtains.
Alfie wonders
if he went downstairs
whether they'd let him stay up, too,
just for a little while.

From *The Big Alfie and Annie Rose Storybook* by Shirley Hughes (Red Fox, 1990)

GO BACK TO BED!

So Alfie _____

_____

MAKE IT COME TRUE!

Dear Fairy Godmother,
I have heard that you might
be able to grant me a wish.

My special wish is

I'm asking you to grant my wish because

I hope that

With love from

_____

BOXED IN!

A better way would be to:

because

Scholastic
NON-FICTION WRITING
Workshop

THE NEW PET

Is this the best way for the giraffe to travel?

SAVE THIS TREE

'But there's nothing wrong with it,' said
Katy. 'It's a lovely tree!'

'My dad says the roots are growing
underneath the wall and making it go all
wobbly. And it's his wall and his tree,
so he can do what he likes, so there.'

He picked up his bag and swaggered
off, looking so like his dad, I felt like
hitting him.

But Steve's attention had been caught by
something quite different: 'Hey! Someone's
been drawing on our tree!'

He was right. There was a big yellow
cross painted on the trunk.

'I wonder why,' said Katy.

'It's so George knows which one to cut
down,' said Small.

We all turned and stared at him.

'Cut down Winkie's Tree,' said Katy.
'He can't!'

'Yes, he can,' said Small. 'With an axe
and a saw and a digger to get the roots
out, only the digger can't come till Friday
week.'

From Save This Tree! by Maggie Pearson (Hodder & Stoughton, 1991)

DARK IS GOOD

because _____

_____

_____

_____

because _____

_____

_____

_____

because _____

_____

_____

_____

We are not afraid and neither should you be, Plop.

KEEP TIGERS IN THE JUNGLE (1)

KEEP TIGERS IN THE JUNGLE (2)

WOULD YOU RATHER ...?

or your mum had a row in a cafe

Would you rather . . . .

your dad did a dance at school

From *Would you Rather?* by John Burningham (Collins Picture Lions, 1994)

PLEASE DON'T

Dear _____,

I am writing to ask you not to _____

_____

I have three good reasons for asking you not to do this.

These are

1. because _____

_____

_____

2. because _____

_____

_____

3. because _____

_____

_____

So please don't.

Love,

_____

CHIPS AND THE CAT

But when Chips told his mum, she didn't think having Chico was a good idea at all. A big argument started.

But you've got a cat already— surely that's enough?

It's only for a week, Mum!

We've got nowhere to put him!

I can have him in my bedroom.

Your BEDROOM! With all that sawdust and mess? You certainly can't keep him in there!

In the shed, then?

The cat might get in there and eat him. No, it's too much RESPONSIBILITY.

But I've told them at school I'm going to look after Chico. I can't go UN-telling them now!

You should have asked me first.

PLEASE, Mum!

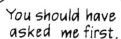

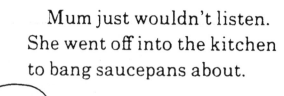

Mum just wouldn't listen. She went off into the kitchen to bang saucepans about.

NO!

from Chips and Jessie by Shirley Hughes (Harper Collins, 1985)

Scholastic
NON-FICTION WRITING
Workshop

NAME

READ THIS BOOK

You should read this book

because

❋

❋

❋

THE MISSING PIECES (1)

To: The Jolly Jigsaw Company

Date: _____

Dear _____

We are writing to complain about _____

_____

When we tried the jigsaw _____

_____

We _____

_____

Please _____

_____

_____

Yours _____

THE MISSING PIECES (2)

The Jolly Jigsaw Company
Puzzle House
West Way
Sawbridge
SW2 3NL

[date as postmark]

Dear Class,

Thank you for your letter.

We are sorry to hear that you were not able to complete our jigsaw because some of the pieces were missing.

We check every jigsaw before it leaves our factory, but sometimes mistakes are made.

Please accept our apologies.

We enclose the missing pieces, which should allow you to complete the jigsaw. We hope that you will enjoy doing so.

With best wishes,

Jim Smith
Production Manager

BIG? BAD? WHO, ME?

TOENAILS

Toenails

More and more people in Britain today are using
TOENAILS

Smart and smooth
they grow
on all five toes of each foot.

We spoke to Jack Davis of Hackney:
'Yes, I like toenails.
I've got ten of them.
Big ones for the big toes
and little ones for the little toes.
They're great.'

Be like Jack.
Be smart.
Grow toenails.

by Michael Rosen (from *The Hypnotiser*, Harper Collins, 1990)

PRODUCTS

hair		eyebrows	
ears		nostrils	
lips		tongue	
knees		elbows	
fingers		neck	
toes		shampoo	
lipstick		toothpaste	
perfume		cakes	
apples		raisins	
ribbons		socks	
gloves		pyjamas	

Scholastic
NON-FICTION WRITING
Workshop

A RADIO ADVERT FOR ...

More and more people in Britain today

are using

_____

_____ and _____

they _____

_____

We spoke to _____ _____ of _____:

'Yes, I like _____.

I've got _____ of them.

_____ ones for _____

and _____ ones for _____ .

They're _____ .'

Be like _____ .

Be smart _____ .

Get _____ .

ON AIR

OUR SCHOOL TRIP

Dear _____

We are planning our school trip.

Can you tell us whether _____

_____

Do you have _____

Is there _____

How much _____

When _____

Our class is _____

We _____

When _____

Please _____

_____

Thank you for your help.

Yours faithfully,

_____

PET EVALUATION SHEET

Pet's name: _____

Good points	Bad points

So I would say this would make a good/bad pet.

Do/Don't get it.

SPECIAL OFFER

Ideas for pictures

Ideas for words

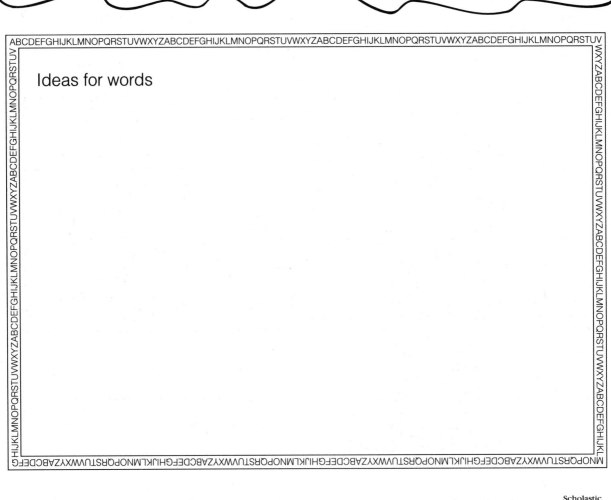

EVALUATION OF AN ADVERT

_____ and _____s advert	Yes	No
Words clear		
Bright and attractive		
Good picture		
Would you buy the sandwich?		

A GREAT DAY OUT

For a great day out visit

THE CHILDREN'S MUSEUM

FACE PAINTING

ROCKING HORSE

COMPUTERS

ELECTRIC TRAINS

DOLLS FROM AROUND THE WORLD

CONSTRUCTION KITS

TOYS FROM VICTORIAN TIMES

SCRAPS

WHEN?
Tuesday to Sunday
10.00 to 6.00 p.m
(Closed Monday)

WHERE?
116 Dandelion Lane
Train Town

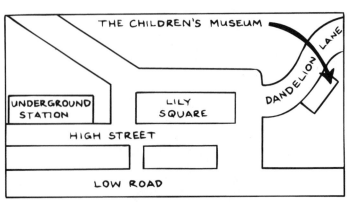

COME AND SEE!

You need to think about:

Title

What will persuade people to come?

Children

Adults

What other information would help?

OAT CRISPIES OR RICE FLAKES

Design Brief for a New Cereal

The name will be printed like this:

The picture will show:

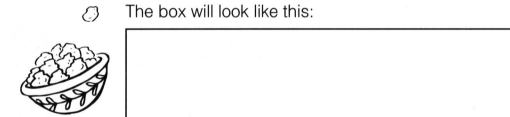
The box will look like this:

Scholastic
WORKSHOP

Chapter Five

INSTRUCTIONS
AND DIRECTIONS

INTRODUCTION

Procedural writing includes **instructions, directions, orders and rules**. It is concerned with 'telling people':

- to or not to
  eg **Stop** or **Do not enter**;
- how to
  for example, use a telephone;
- where to
  for example, find the railway station.

This chapter features many of the 'one-item' instructions which are a familiar feature of life in the early years at school, such as 'Draw three apples.' 'Please wash your hands.' 'Be quiet in the library.' It also deals with more complex sets of instructions:

- recipes, for example how to make a sandwich;
- instructions for using equipment, such as a photocopier or a video recorder;
- how to make something, such as a birthday card or a LEGO model;
- how to play a game, such as dominoes;
- how to find something, such as buried treasure;
- how to order something, such as a pizza;
- how to get somewhere, for example to school.

Why is procedural writing important?

This kind of writing is frequently used in everyday life. Children are thus likely to be familiar with many situations in which instructions and directions are required. They can immediately see the purpose of learning how to give clear directions to a place or how to instruct others in the correct way of doing something. These are skills which will enable them to function effectively in adult life, but which are also required during childhood.

Children need to be able to follow instructions and directions in order to cross the street safely, apply for a free gift, play dominoes, build a model with Meccano, and so on. They often need to present clear instructions and directions to peers and adults – for example, how to play a game or get to a friend's house.

Instructions and directions are also needed throughout children's school years, in terms of the general life of the establishment (for example, how to find the gymnasium or buy lunch) and in terms of curriculum studies (for example, how to use the school library or make a model). In the classroom, children are given many spoken instructions and directions to follow. Written instructions will increasingly play a role in education through workcards and worksheets and through detailed rules and routines in the classroom and beyond.

To learn about their world and to function effectively in society, children have to be able both to interpret and to give instructions and directions, and to recognise a variety of styles and purposes for these kinds of writing.

What children know about instructions and directions

Most children coming to school will already be aware of instructions and directions in the form of signs: no entry, no litter, no smoking, a map of a woodland walk, directions for getting to the library, and so on. Anyone who travels with and listens to young children will know that their attention is often drawn to such things –

'What does that say, Dad?', 'What does that picture mean?', 'No, that's the boys' toilet'. The last two of these illustrate children's awareness that not only writing but also pictures can be used to send messages.

Children aged five or six already have experience of giving and receiving instructions and directions, especially in spoken language. In the home setting, they may be used to being asked to 'Tidy up your toys' or 'Wash and dry your hands before tea'. Home experiences of following recipes, washing instructions or directions on packets may also have given them some experience of written instructions. In the wider world, they may have gained knowledge of the sequence of events in everyday situations such as using a car wash, buying a lottery ticket or ordering a pizza. In play situations, children can be heard trying to direct their own and other children's behaviour and activities. 'You need wet sand to fill the bucket. Then you tip it up really quickly and pat the top with a spade. Lift it up and you have a sandcastle.'

However, children's awareness of instructions and directions (oral, written or pictorial) will be very varied, and will depend on whether adults (at home or in the nursery) have given explanations and encouraged them to take part in activities and to ask questions. In any class, the teacher will find that pupils have had very different experiences in the years before coming to school, and should recognise that they will continue to have diverse experiences in their lives outside the school.

KEY FEATURES OF PROCEDURAL WRITING

The key features of instructions and directions are as follows:
• They must serve the **purpose** set. (What am I giving these instructions for?)
• They must be appropriate to the **audience**. (Who are they addressed to?)

These two fundamental aspects underline all the following features of procedural writing:
• It is clear and easy to follow (**coherent**).
• It is short and to the point (**precise** and **concise**).
• It avoids irrelevant material (**relevant**).
• Where appropriate, instructions are given in sequence. They can be numbered.
• Pictures or diagrams may be used.
Instructions are often written in the format:
• title (for example, 'How to Bake a Cake');
• what you need (for example, ingredients);
• what you do (method).
Instructions and directions share these linguistic features:
• They normally use the imperative mood: *Go there. Do this.*
• They are given in chronological order.
• They use words like *first, then, next,* and *finally.*
• They are about action.

LEARNING ABOUT PROCEDURAL WRITING

Awareness of audience and purpose

Children need to learn that how you give an instruction or direction will depend upon who you are giving it to and what you are giving it for. Thus writing instructions for someone in the class (who would be familar with the scenario) is different from writing instructions for a toddler (who would require pictorial material) or for a parent (who might reasonably be expected to be a skilled reader). What the audience/reader brings to the task will influence the writer's decisions about format and style. The writer needs to consider:
• How much does this reader already know?
• How much do I need to tell her/him?

Content and sequence

Children need to learn how to select the essential information first, before arranging it in an order appropriate to the writing task.

Using familiar contexts (examples in this book include ordering a pizza, writing rules for a game of dominoes and creating directions for finding hidden treasure) supports children by allowing them to work with familiar content. This means that they can focus on the key learning elements of the writing task (such as sequencing instructions), rather than on the content of what is being written.

Many young children find putting events in chronological order a difficult task. They can be helped to develop this skill by activities which involve sequencing pictures, putting a known sequence of instructions into the correct order or sorting mixed-up instructions into their correct sets (see activities 2, 5, 6, 9, 14 and 21 in this chapter).

Structural features

Children are quick to notice similarities and differences between different formats, and can be encouraged to see patterns. The format of a recipe or 'How to make a ...' is an important general structure which, once grasped, can be transferred to many new situations. The photocopiable sheets included in this chapter provide useful examples of various formats.

Key words

Children need to learn various key words which help with sequencing, such as *first, second, third, next, then, finally* and *last*. They also need to learn how to phrase instructions and directions by using action words (verbs):

First **wash** your hands.

Take two slices of bread.

Spread them with butter or margarine.

Arrange lettuce, egg and tomato on one slice.

Add some mayonnaise.

Put the other slice on top.

To develop this awareness, children need to be given opportunities to analyse and criticise examples of procedural writing which they are using (such as recipes or the rules for games), and to analyse their own and each other's talk and writing.

Pictures and diagrams

Young children are accustomed to 'reading' pictures and diagrams, and using context clues to make sense of writing. (At this level, they may not distinguish clearly between a picture and a diagram.) Focusing on the way that a picture or sequence of pictures gives information is an important activity. The children can then begin to decide where and when they could use pictures and diagrams as part of their own writing. They need to consider:

• Will I need writing or just pictures?

• Which pictures do I need?

• How can I create these pictures – by drawing, by using photographs?

• What information do the pictures give?

Clarity and coherence

Children need to learn that clarity and comprehensiveness are essential if the reader is to follow written instructions. This point can be made by basing the writing task on a real experience (such as using a photocopier), and then encouraging the children (before they start writing) to talk through what they did and how they did it. A child's writing can be tested for clarity and coherence by passing it to another child, who follows the instructions and then gives feedback to the writer.

Being precise and concise can be difficult for young children, who sometimes want to include everything that may happen and sometimes just give the bare minimum, missing out important points. The teacher can support the children's writing by:

• talking about the subject before they start writing about it;

• involving them in activities which require them to select and discard things;

• asking questions such as:

– *Is that really important to what we are doing/ talking about now?*

– *Do Class 3 really need to know that the cold water felt warm the day we did our floating and sinking experiment?*

Linking with reading

Through their experience of writing instructions and directions, children should become more aware of how to read and use them effectively. Conversely, reading and using instructions and directions helps to make children aware of which formats, styles and words are effective. It is thus important to maintain close links between reading and writing activities.

How can procedural writing be taught?

Teachers should be aware of the following points.

• Children need to talk about their knowledge and experience of instructions, directions, orders and rules.

• Children also need to recall events, activities and processes in sequence and talk about them to appreciate the function of procedural writing.

• The teacher needs to take account of the children's interests and experience when selecting contexts for procedural writing.

• Activities should give children opportunities to decide on the most appropriate way to give instructions and directions to a particular audience for a particular purpose.

• The children should use real resources (such as recipes and examples of environmental print) for real purposes, creating material which will be used by real audiences.

• It is important to find contexts in which giving and receiving instructions and directions 'comes naturally' and is intrinsic to the situation. This will occur in many different curriculum areas; in play situations such as the café, shop, hairdresser's salon or dentist's surgery; and during exploration of sand, water, clay and other natural materials.

• The teacher needs to provide situations in which children experience a variety of groupings – class, groups, pairs and individuals – in order to develop their awareness of the audience for instructions and directions.

• The teacher also needs to identify teaching points which will make children aware of the key features of procedural texts (see above).

Organisation of this chapter

The 21 activities in this chapter focus on the key features of instructions and directions, and are organised as follows: 1–4, Awareness of audience and purpose; 5–10, Sequence and structure; 11–16, The words we use; 17–21, Pictures and diagrams.

In many of the activities, it is suggested that the teacher start by working with the whole class, focusing on key teaching points (such as selection of content, sequencing, key words or the need for illustration) and modelling the task for the children. Paired, individual or group work, giving practice in the particular skills which have been introduced, follows. These sessions provide opportunities for children to share their ideas to test whether their instructions and directions actually work. Having a 'real' purpose will make the children's task much clearer to them.

Activity	Teaching content	Star rating	Group size	Photo-copiable
AUDIENCE AND PURPOSE				
1 Rules for the sand area	Rules should be short, sensible and clear. The most important rule can be stated first.	*	(W) ⇨ 4	✓
2 How to play dominoes	Games have rules, which need to be understood by everyone playing.	**	4 ⇨ (W) ⇨ 4	✓
3 How to make a birthday card	Writing instructions requires practical knowledge.	*/**	4	✓
4 Find the treasure	Directions can be spoken, written down or shown on a map or plan.	***	(W) ⇨ 2	✓✓
SEQUENCE AND STRUCTURE				
5 Mixed-up instructions	Writing a sequence using numbered steps.	*	4	✓
6 How to order a pizza by phone	Prioritising information, then sequencing instructions.	**	(W) ⇨ 1	✓
7 Lost in a forest	Using clear, simple and logical language to give directions.	**/***	(W) ⇨ 2 ⇨ (W)	✓✓
8 How to make a LEGO tower	Using a flow chart to give instructions.	*	1 ⇨ 4	✓
9 Recipe for boy soup	Recipes are usually given in the form of a title, ingredients and method.	**	(W) ⇨ 4	✓✓✓
10 How to operate a video recorder	Written instructions are useful if clear and in a sequence of numbered steps.	**	4 ⇨ (W) ⇨ 2	✓✓
THE WORDS WE USE				
11 Telling words	Using action words to write instructions.	*	(W) ⇨ 1	✓
12 How to choose	Adding detail to a given instruction to make it more specific.	**	(W) ⇨ 1 ⇨ (W)	✓✓
13 Our own rules	Rules often begin with an action word. They can be sequenced in order of importance.	***	(W) ⇨ 2 ⇨ (W)	✓
14 The big breakfast	A set of instructions can be given in words and pictures. Both must be in sequence.	*	(W) ⇨ 4 ⇨ 1	✓
15 My route to school	Directions use a particular language. Pictures, maps and plans can help.	***	4 ⇨ 2 ⇨ 4	✓
16 Say it with pictures	Using pictures to represent the action words in instructions.	*	(W) ⇨ 1	✓
PICTURES AND DIAGRAMS				
17 Warning signs	Road signs use pictures and shapes to convey messages.	*/**	(W) ⇨ 1 ⇨ 2	✓✓
18 Paint mixing	Pictures in a sequence can convey a series of instructions.	*/**	(W) ⇨ 2	✓✓
19 Don't do that	A simple pictorial sign can tell us **not** to do something.	*/**	(W) ⇨ 1 ⇨ (W)	✓✓
20 At the airport	Signs can give instructions and directions, as well as information.	**	(W) ⇨ 4	✓
21 Recipe for a sandwich	The sequence of words and pictures in a recipe gives instructions.	*	4 ⇨ 2	✓✓
			(W) = whole group	

Scholastic
NON-FICTION WRITING
Workshop

RULES FOR THE SAND AREA

Teaching content

Rules can be indicated by words or pictures. Rules should be short, sensible and clear. The most important rule can be stated first.

What you need

Photocopiable page 147; scissors; A4 sheets of paper, drawing materials; large sheets of sugar paper, adhesive.

What to do

Explain to the children that the next day, you will be adding the sand trough and equipment to the play area or room. If the children have used a sand area before, ask them if they can remember how they kept it safe and tidy. Encourage them to think about:

1. What things might it be dangerous to do with sand? Refer to their experiences at the seaside or at nursery. Their answers will probably include: throwing sand at people (it could go in their eyes); throwing sand around the floor (people could slip); eating sand (it could make you ill). Note the children's answers for later use.

2. What will we need to keep the sand area tidy? Answers should include:
• a dustpan and brush;
• a place to put all the things we play with.

NEVER TH... ...PEOPLE

Emphasise the further points that when we have finished with the sand, we should:
• sweep sand up from the floor;
• put all the equipment back on the shelf/rack in the right place, so that it is ready for other people.

Ask the children whether it is possible for us all to play in the sand at the same time. Why not? What would happen if we tried? They should conclude that numbers will have to be limited. Ask them: *How many should be allowed?* They will probably say about four. *So how can we tell people this?* They should suggest making a rule that only four can play in the sand.

Recap all the rules discussed so far. These should include:

Never throw sand at people.

Never throw sand on the floor.

Never eat sand.

Always brush the floor when you have finished.

Tidy up the toys after you.

Only four can play here.

Explain to the children that they are now going to draw pictures to go with these rules, to make them clearer to everyone who uses the sand area. Explore with them what illustrations might be effective. They might suggest a picture of a child eating sand for *Never eat sand,* or a tidy box of toys for *Tidy up the toys after you.* Ask them how a picture can indicate something *not* to be done. Introduce the idea that on many signs which tell people not to do something, they will see a red line crossing a picture. Suggest that they might like to use this for their own No/Never signs.

Organise the class into groups of six children. Give one copy of the 'Sand rules' sheet (page 147) to each group. Ask them to divide up the drawing task between them by cutting up the rules and sharing them out.

When the drawings have been completed, give each group a large sheet of sugar paper or card on which to display their rules. Encourage them to choose a suitable order for the rules, and to match pictures to words in a clear way.

One or two sets of rules can be placed at the sand area. Others could be taken to other classes who use the sand area; children from your class could explain the rules and the reasons for them to the other classes.

Further development

A similar procedure could be followed to establish rules for the use of any working or play area in the classroom (such as the gluing area, painting area or jigsaw table) or in and around the school (such as the gymnasium, the dining hall or the playground).

HOW TO PLAY DOMINOES

Teaching content

Games have rules, which need to be clear and understood by everyone playing.

What you need

Sets of dominoes; large sheets of newsprint, marker pens; photocopiable sheet 148, scissors, adhesive, strips of card; A4 paper, drawing materials; large sheets of card.

What to do

Organise the class so that they are seated in groups of four to six children. Each group receives a set of dominoes to play with. (These could be picture dominoes, colour, word or number dominoes.) Ask the groups to play with the dominoes in the usual way.

When each game is completed, ask the children if they had any problems in playing the game. Did they all play it in the same way? Did anyone have a different way? The children should mention the need for rules – everybody has to play by the same rules or follow the same instructions.

Explain to the children that the Reception or P1 class(es) don't know the rules for dominoes yet. Could the children help them with this by producing a set of rules for them to follow? Give each group a large sheet of newsprint and ask them to write down or draw a picture of each rule they can think of. The children should come up with the following:

- Take it in turns.
- Share out the dominoes – same number to each player.
- Match your domino to one on the ends of the line.
- Knock on the table if you can't take a turn.
- The winner is the first person to have no dominoes left unplaced.

Bring the sheets together to show to the whole class and talk through the procedure in steps, using the children's ideas. Write a number for each step as you go along.

Give each group a copy of the rule sheet (page 148). Explain that the children have to decide which order the five instruction steps should go in. They have to cut out the steps, put them in order, number them, then glue the number and the rule onto a strip of card. Give each group six strips of card (including one for the title).

When they have finished, ask the children whether the Reception/P1 class would understand these rules. The children should realise that the Reception/P1 children cannot read and may need pictures to help them. Each child in the group should then select a rule or instruction and draw a picture (on an A4 sheet) to express it. The illustrated rules or instructions should then be mounted on a large sheet of card. The groups' completed rule sheets can then be presented to the Reception/P1 class(es).

Further development

The children could make sets of dominoes for the younger class and draw smaller instructions to go with these (perhaps inventing new rules).

HOW TO MAKE A BIRTHDAY CARD

✳✳✳ 𝍢𝍢 (30)→(30)

Teaching content

Writing instructions for an activity requires practical knowledge of the activity as well as awareness of purpose and audience.

What you need

A variety of commercial birthday cards; sheets of card, marker pens, picture-making materials, scissors, glue sticks; a chalkboard or large sheet of paper; word cards (see below); photocopiable page 149.

What to do

This activity fits well with the everyday life of a class, in which the celebration of birthdays is a regular occurrence. (However, if you are aware of children who do not celebrate birthdays for religious reasons, a different occasion should be considered.) The two parts of the activity could be run either in separate sessions or 'end-on'. The card-making could be a choosing time activity, with the instruction writing following at worktime.

1. Making birthday cards

Group four to six children at a work table and look briefly at some commercial birthday cards to establish that they are folded, with a picture on the front part and a written greeting inside. Note the different styles of different cards, and ask the children to think about why this is.

Their response should help you to establish the importance of **audience**: who will receive the card – a friend, parent, grandparent and so on.

Tell the children that they are going to design and make a card for the person of their choice. Introduce card-making materials and discuss the procedure:

1. Select a piece of card and fold it. (Different folds produce different shapes.)
2. Draw or choose a picture for the front. (Think about the person who will receive it. What would he/she like?)
3. Write a greeting inside. (Scribe some useful words and phrases on a chalkboard or large sheet of paper.)

When the cards are finished, take a little time to discuss them with the group; then let them show their cards to the rest of the class. Suggest that the group could write instructions to help others do this activity successfully.

2. Instruction writing

Gather the same group together at the writing table. Each child should have the card which he/she made earlier. Also have to hand the card-making materials and tools, and provide a set of appropriate word cards (such as **paper**, **coloured**, **scissors**, **picture**, **draw**, **stick**, **inside**, **front**).

Remind the children that they are going to write instructions to help their friends make similar cards. (This establishes the purpose and audience.) First, ask them to think about what their friends will need to know. *What should we tell them?* Note their ideas on the chalkboard. Then ask them to recall their activity. *How did you make your card? What did you do first? And then?* Agree on a sequence of actions.

Introduce the card-making instruction sheet (page 149) and discuss the headings given as well as how to word the instructions (action words first). Model this using word cards. Remind the children that what they write should be clear and simple.

Each child should now complete photocopiable page 149. Sheets can be exchanged within the group before being tested by other children. Are any revisions necessary? The children may wish to add diagrams to make the instructions clearer.

Further development

The children could send their completed cards to their friends and family members. They could write instructions on how to make an envelope, address an envelope or post a letter; or they could modify their card-making instructions for other types of card, such as Christmas or Diwali cards.

Children could test and review simple craft books which provide instructions, and give them a rating for clarity (perhaps on a scale of 1 to 3).

4

FIND THE TREASURE

★★★ Ⓦ →🚹🚹 ⏱60

Teaching content

Directions can be spoken, written down for other people to follow or shown using key features on a picture, map or plan.

What you need

Enlarged (A3) copies of photocopiable page 150; plastic model figures (preferably pirates); photocopiable page 151, cut or torn into pieces; A4 paper, adhesive; writing materials (if needed).

What to do

Explain to the children that they are pirates. Their task is to explain to Pirate Pam how to get from the harbour to the treasure, which is marked with a cross on the treasure map. The original instructions for finding the treasure have been lost.

Divide the class into pairs, and give each pair an A3 copy of the treasure map (page 150) and a small plastic 'pirate' figure. Ask them to guide the figure across the map to the treasure by a sensible route, discussing the stages of the route with each other.

When the children have worked out their route, tell them that the instructions to find the treasure have been found – but someone has torn them up. Can the children, working in pairs, help to put the instructions together in the right order? Give each pair a torn-up or cut-up copy of photocopiable page 151. When they have reassembled and checked the instructions, they should stick them down in the correct order on a sheet of A4 paper. Some children may prefer to write out their own set of instructions and check these against the given set.

Further development

Making model layouts and classroom friezes provides children with opportunities to practise giving directions. For example, if the children have created a 'dinosaur museum' in the classroom (as suggested in Chapter 7 of the Key Stage 1 *Non-Fiction Writing Projects* book), they could make maps and signs showing visitors where to find the exhibits, café, toilets, exit, and so on.

MIXED-UP INSTRUCTIONS

Teaching content

Instructions must be clear, sensible and written in sequence. A sequence can be written using numbered steps.

What you need

Photocopiable page 152; a large sheet of paper divided into four boxes and labelled *Recipe for chocolate cake, How to get to the assembly hall, How to use the video, How to play Snakes and Ladders*; adhesive or Blu-tack, scissors.

What to do

To create the context for this activity, tell a group of six to eight children that recently you were busy writing:
• a recipe for chocolate cake (to give to another teacher);
• directions to the assembly hall (for a child who is new to school);
• instructions for using the video (in case you forget);
• the rules for Snakes and Ladders (to give to another class).

Explain that somehow all of these have become mixed up. Can the children help you sort them out? Show the group a copy of

photocopiable page 152 and a large sheet of blank paper with the titles written in four separate boxes.

Read, or let the children read, the instructions under *Recipe for chocolate cake* on the photocopiable sheet. Decide whether each instruction makes sense under this title – and if not, which title it should belong under and why. Cut around the misplaced instructions and select children to stick or Blu-tack them into the appropriate box, in the right order, on the large sheet of paper. The children should now read them back to check that they make sense. Repeat this with each of the other mixed-up sets of instructions, until they are all in the right boxes and in the right order. Thank the children for being so helpful and solving the problem.

HOW TO ORDER A PIZZA BY PHONE

Teaching content

Deciding what information is important or not important for a task. Prioritising information, then sequencing instructions in a logical order.

What you need

Photocopiable page 153, scissors, Blu-tack; two large sheets of paper (one with headings as in Figure 1), a marker pen.

What to do

Start by asking the class if anyone in their homes has ever ordered a pizza by phone. If so, who ordered it and what did they have to do? If the children have not had this experience, ask them to predict some of the steps they might take to obtain the pizza. Record some of their suggestions on a large sheet of paper.

Give each child a copy of photocopiable page 153. Suggest that the ten instructions listed on the sheet are things you might do when ordering a pizza by phone. Ask the children to cut out each instruction. Discuss the instructions and compare them with the class list. Show the children a large sheet with the headings *Important* and *Not important* (see Figure 1). Discuss whether each of the

instructions is important. Select individual children to come out and Blu-tack each instruction in the appropriate column. Ask the others whether they agree or disagree and why.

Important	Not important

Figure 1

When all of the ten instructions have been discussed, focus the children's attention on the *Important* column and ask them to suggest which action they would do first. Work through the sequence, at each stage reinforcing why an instruction comes just after the previous one. Read out the final list of instructions. Ask the children whether they think that this list will work if you follow it through, step by step. The children should now glue their instructions, in the correct order, onto a piece of paper.

It would be appropriate to carry this through in reality with the children, and arrange for a small group to order a pizza and either collect it or have it delivered to the school. **NB** Make sure the children understand that they should not order a pizza (or anything else) by phone without prior adult agreement!

To complete this activity, the children could draw pictures for different instructions; these could then be collated on a frieze with the title *How to order a pizza by phone.*

LOST IN A FOREST

Teaching content
The language used in giving directions has to be clear and simple. The directions must follow a logical sequence.

What you need
Photocopiable pages 154 and 155, scissors, writing materials.

What to do
Divide the class into pairs. Give each pair a copy of the Forest Guide sheet (photocopiable page 154). Ask them to read the words on each of the squares (or use the pictures to guess what each says). Explain that the words and signs will give Little Red Riding Hood some information about what she can and can't do as she tries to make her way from her house to Grandma's cottage. Pose this as a challenge to the children: *Little Red Riding Hood needs to find her way through the woods to Grandma's cottage. How can she get there? Where should she go first? Could there be more than one way?*

First of all, each pair needs to cut out the picture of Little Red Riding Hood. Starting at her house, and using the cut-out character, the children should work out a route for her to get safely to Grandma's cottage. (They can 'track' the route via the squares on the Forest Guide.) When you feel that all the children have made an attempt at discussing alternative routes, stop

Scholastic
NON-FICTION WRITING
Workshop

the class and ask some of the pairs to offer their suggestions orally to the others.

For the last part of the activity, give each pair a copy of photocopiable page 155 and explain that you now want each pair to write a letter to Little Red Riding Hood, giving instructions based on their previous discussion. Depending on their ability, the children may choose to write words or draw symbols or pictures, or use a combination of these forms. Whatever form is chosen, each should be valued by the teacher. Tell the children that to help them write the instructions in order, they may use words such as *first* and *then*, or use numbers (1, 2, 3...), or write one instruction on each line.

Finally, bring the whole class back together. Ask for some pairs to volunteer to show their letters to the rest of the class. It would be useful for one of the pair to indicate the route on the Forest Guide as the other child reads out the letter written to Little Red Riding Hood..

Children's letters could be displayed on a frieze entitled 'How to get Little Red Riding Hood to Grandma's cottage', with a background of trees and wolves.

Further development
This activity could be linked to other traditional stories; for example, the children could help Hansel and Gretel to escape through the wood, or help the Musicians of Bremen to find the empty house.

8

HOW TO MAKE A LEGO TOWER

Teaching content
How to use a flow chart to give instructions.

What you need
A collection of LEGO bricks; a camera (to take photographs of LEGO towers); photocopiable page 156, writing and drawing materials.

What to do
This activity requires you to work with some children on an individual basis before others can be involved. Ask one child to build up a tower using six LEGO bricks of any colour. In the early stages, you may structure the use of the bricks by providing only those with eight

connecting studs (in various colours). When the tower has been built, take a photograph of the finished product with the name of the child who built it displayed alongside. Repeat this with another five children (one at a time) to build up a small bank of photographs showing different towers.

When each photo has been developed, show it to the child whose tower is shown and ask her/him to think about how she/he could tell others how to make it. Talk about each brick in turn, using words such as *first, put, then, on top, last.*

Show the child the sequence frames on photocopiable page 156. Ask her/him to draw the brick that was put down first in the first large box on the sheet. Then ask the child to write the first instruction in the space underneath – either by writing or by drawing, or with you scribing. The emphasis in this part of the activity is on the process of giving instructions to other children, not on recounting how the tower was made. Encourage the use of the words provided on the photocopiable sheet.

Continue with this sequence until the child has drawn each brick and the instruction for each stage has been written/drawn in. Finally, ask the child to check that the instructions match the photograph of the tower.

Now involve a small group of other children by showing them one of the sets of instructions. Ask them to make the tower by following these instructions. When they have finished, show them the corresponding photograph and ask: *Does your tower look like ....'s?*

This is a fairly simple activity, but it allows you to ask the children to evaluate the instructions they are given – *Were they easy to follow? Did they tell you the steps in the right order?* You can use this type of activity for more complex tasks, with a greater number of children writing more extended instructions for a variety of models (depending on age and ability).

9

RECIPE FOR BOY SOUP

Teaching content
Recipes are usually given in the form of a title, ingredients and method. The method is often a numbered sequence of instructions.

What you need
Photocopiable pages 157 and 158; photocopiable page 159 with instructions cut out; spreaders, paste, drawing materials.

What to do
Read the recipe for Boy Soup* on photocopiable page 157 to the class, and hand out the recipe sheet for them to look at. Point out to them that recipes are generally written in this format:
• **Title** – This tells us what we are going to make. *Why is this important?*
• **Ingredients** – This list tells us what we will need to have before starting. *Why is this important?*

• **Method** – This tells us what to do; the instructions are sometimes numbered. *Why is this important?*

The children could look at other recipes in recipe books to see whether this pattern is followed. What other headings might they find – equipment, variations, number of servings?

Explain that the wolf did not succeed in making boy soup, because the boy forgot to tell him one vital ingredient. Can the children guess what it might be? The answer is SALT. So the boy was saved. However, the wolf still wants his soup – so decides to make girl soup instead. But his recipe has got all mixed up. Organise the children into mixed-ability groups of four to six, and give each group a mixed-up set of instructions cut from photocopiable page 159. Ask them to work together to sort the recipe into:

title

ingredients

method

Give each group a copy of photocopiable page 158 to provide a framework for their sorting. When they have arranged all the cut-out instructions in the correct order under the correct headings on page 158, they can stick them down to create a permanent recipe sheet. The finished sheets can be illustrated and displayed.

Further development
Particularly skilled writers may be able to write their own recipes for Boy Pie or Girl Pudding, adapting recipes from books.
* From *Beware of Boys* by Tony Blundell (Picture Puffin, 1993).

HOW TO OPERATE A VIDEO RECORDER

Teaching content

Written instructions are most effective if they are clear and presented in a sequence of numbered steps, with illustrations.

What you need

Photocopiable pages 160 and 161; access to a photocopier and a video recorder; A3 paper for photocopying.

What to do

At worktime, give one group a copy of the 'To operate the photocopier' sheet (photocopiable page 160) and ask them to take it to the school office to photocopy. Explain that you need six copies (or one per group – see below), and that you would like them made twice as big as the original (enlarged to A3 size). The children now go to the school office and carry out the task.

Later, gather the class together and give each group one of the A3 copies of page 160. Encourage the children to ask the members of the group which was sent to the office whether they found the task easy:

• Did they follow the instructions on the sheet?
• Did the instructions help them take the copies?
• What features of the instructions helped?
• What was difficult?
• Was anything that was necessary missing from the instruction sheet?

Children in the group who used the photocopier should mention:
• The numbers helped.
• The pictures made the instructions clearer.
• The instructions were simple to read and carry out.
• There weren't lots of words.
• **BUT** they didn't tell us how to make something bigger!

Explain that these instructions were meant to help with simple photocopying, not the more complicated task the group were asked to carry out.

Tell the children that lots of teachers in the school need instructions to help them work machines. One machine which teachers often have trouble with is the video recorder. Explore with the children their experiences of using video recorders at home. Which children have learned how to do this? Was it easy to learn? It may become evident that some parents could also do with instructions to help them work the video recorder. (If necessary, use the school video recorder in the classroom as a preparation for this activity.)

Pair the children and ask those with the relevant knowledge to explain to each other:
1. How to record a programme.
2. How to play back a recorded video.

Give a copy of the 'To operate the video recorder' sheet (photocopiable page 161) to each pair. Ask them to complete the written instructions, following the pattern in the 'To operate the photocopier' sheet. Completed instruction sheets may be exchanged and tested by other children. If agreement is reached on an effective instruction sheet, this could be copied and issued to staff members (who should be encouraged to give feedback).

TELLING WORDS

Teaching content

When writing instructions, begin with action words (such as *put, look at, stop, pick up*).

What you need

A chalkboard or large sheet of paper; photocopiable page 162, writing and drawing materials; scissors, adhesive, backing paper.

What to do

Start by gathering the class together and asking the children to think about all the things you tell them to do in the classroom: *pick up all the paper from the floor, put away your books, tidy the ..., look at ..., don't ..., stop ...* and so on. List these action words on a chalkboard or large sheet of paper, and explain to the children that these are some of the **doing words** we will use if we are saying or writing instructions.

Now give each child a copy of photocopiable page 162. Explain that first of all, you want each child to write three things that her/his dad, mum or gran tells her/him to do in the speech bubbles. You may have to scribe for some children. Then ask each child to draw a picture of her/himself and a friend, and write two things that she/he tells her/his friend to do, on the second part of the sheet.

Bring the children back together and compare some of the instructions they have written. It would be useful to cut out some of the pictures and speech bubbles to create a collage of 'Things We Tell People to Do'. This could also include some creative children's drawings of you giving instructions.

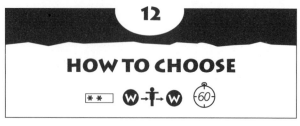

HOW TO CHOOSE

Teaching content

Detail can be added to a given instruction to make it more specific.

What you need

Photocopiable pages 163 and 164, writing and drawing materials; a large sheet of paper with 'new toy' written in the middle, a marker pen.

What to do

Gather the class together and give each child a copy of photocopiable page 163, 'Choosing Your Cat'*. Ask the children whether they have ever gone to choose a pet from a pet shop or choose a puppy or kitten from a litter. Look again at the cat picture and discuss each of the features that the authors say they would look for. Ask the children: *What makes a good pet?*

Now put up a large sheet of paper and tell the children that you want them to think about what they would look for if they were choosing a friend. Would it involve the same things as looking for a good pet? Take some suggestions and write these around the words 'new friend'. The children might suggest:

- plays with you;
- is happy all the time;
- doesn't fight with you;
- shares toys with you.

Tell the children that they may choose to write about choosing a new pet **or** choosing a new friend. Give them the blank photocopiable page 163, and ask them to draw a picture of the pet or friend in the box provided. This will give you some time to talk with individuals. Ask the children to label five things they would look for and write these around their picture in the boxes provided. Scribe for them where necessary.

When the children have finished, bring them back together as a class to share their ideas. Their completed photocopiable sheets could then be collated in two books entitled *How to Choose a Pet* and *How to Choose a Friend*, which could be added to the class library.

This activity could lend itself to a variety of other contexts, for example choosing a good toy, choosing a little brother or choosing a favourite menu.

* From *How To Look After Your Cat* by Colin and Jacqui Hawkins (Walker Books, 1982).

13

OUR OWN RULES

*** ⓦ→🚹→ⓦ ㊺

Teaching content

Children can use action words to write simple rules for the use of a classroom area, in the form of a numbered list. The rules can be sequenced according to the relative importance of the tasks to be carried out.

What you need

A chalkboard or large sheet of paper; photocopiable page 165, writing and drawing materials.

What to do

Establish that the children understand rules as a set of instructions. Talk generally about the kinds of rules you have in the classroom or the school, and why they exist. This activity will

have most relevance at the start of a new term, when rules need to be revised or when a new classroom area is being established.

Gather the class together and set the context for this activity – for example:

• *The Home Corner is always in a mess. We need some rules to keep it tidy.*

• *We are going to set up a café, but we need rules about what will happen there.*

• *We can't all go out of the classroom at once – what rules should we have for lining up and going out?*

Ask the children to talk in pairs (or threes) and decide on a single rule to feed back to the class. Remind them that their rule will probably begin with an action word such as *put, stand, keep, share* or *decide*. It may even be preceded by *Please*.

As each pair feeds back a rule, write the suggestions on a chalkboard or large sheet of paper for all the children to see. Look for similarities between the children's suggestions and, with them, try to refine the wording so that the rules are simple and concise. You may also wish to discuss which rules are most important, and to sequence the rules accordingly.

Finally, ask the children to work in their pairs (or threes) to design a list of the rules you have been discussing. This should take the form of a numbered sequence. The rules can be expressed in writing or by pictorial representation, and with or without teacher scribing, depending on the children's ability. Give each pair a copy of photocopiable page 165 to help them in structuring the task. The children working together should sign their own set of rules, to help them develop an awareness of authorship.

The children's sets of rules could be brought together at a later date so that the class can agree on which set of rules should be displayed in the classroom area. Other contributions could be collated in a class book and left in the relevant area to remind children of the activity.

THE BIG BREAKFAST

Teaching content

A set of instructions can be given in words and pictures. Both must be clear and in sequence. The instructions can be given in a set format such as a recipe, using sequence words such as *first*, *next*, *then* and *finally*.

What you need

One packet of breakfast cereal, milk in a jug, sugar in a container, a bowl, a spoon; six bowls and six spoons; photocopiable page 166, cut into strips; long strips of card or sugar paper; a chalkboard or large sheet of paper.

What to do

Keep the class seated in their usual places, but make sure they can all see you sitting at a table in front of them. Ask them to watch you carefully and quietly while you eat your breakfast. Set the table with: a cereal packet, milk, sugar, one bowl and one spoon.

Sit at the place set and go through the actions: pour the cereal into the bowl, pour milk onto the cereal, sprinkle sugar on top (if required) and eat the cereal. Tell the children that if they were watching carefully, they will now be able to explain to others exactly *what you need* to prepare cereal for breakfast and *what you do* before you can eat it.

On a chalkboard or large sheet of paper, write **What you need**. Take the children's suggestions and write and/or draw them on the board. Explain that in recipes the things that will be eaten are called the *ingredients*; the bowls, spoons and so on are called *utensils* or *equipment*.

Now ask the children what you did *first*. Write FIRST on the board and write one of the children's answers next to it – for example, *First pour the cereal into the bowl*.

Then ask the children: *'And what did I do NEXT?'* Add to chalkboard as above: *Next pour milk onto your cereal*. Continue until you have the full sequence:

- *Then sprinkle sugar on top.*
- *Finally, eat your cereal.*

Read over the sequence with the children and draw their attention to the important sequence words. Explain that you are now going to remove these from the board. You will check later how much the children remember.

Divide the class into six groups. Tell them that one person in each group is going to demonstrate the sequence again. The others in the group have to match and order the instructions from the 'Breakfast' sheet (photocopiable page 166). Give each group a copy of page 166, with the title and four instructions cut out. Allocate the task of demonstrating the sequence, then let the groups carry on. Each group should end up with the instructions in the correct sequence.

Now point out that some people (such as younger children) may not be able to read the instructions. How can they be made clearer?

Figure 2

Could the children draw pictures to help? Issue each child with a long strip of card or sugar paper and show them how to make a four-page zigzag book. (See Figure 2.) They should draw a picture for each step on one page, using the sequenced instructions to help them. Some children may choose to write the words they think are important under each picture.

Further development
This idea can be used for other sequences of actions, such as brushing teeth.

MY ROUTE TO SCHOOL

Teaching content
Directions must be in a particular language and be precise and clear to others. Pictures, maps and plans can help.

What you need
Flashcards with direction words such as *along, across, beside, round, past, near, left, right*; a chalkboard or large sheet of paper; leaflets on various places of interest to visit; photocopiable page 120.

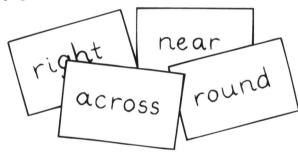

What to do
This lesson would be most effective with a group of six to eight children, delivered as part of a work programme (possibly with a different group each day). It could be linked to the 'Where should we go?' activity on page 91.

Start by describing the route you take to school every day. Accentuate the **direction words**, for example: **Along** the High Street, **across** the road, **beside** the supermarket, **round** the corner at the garage, **past** the sweet shop, then **left** into the school playground.

Could the children understand your directions? What words helped them to understand? The children may identify the special position and direction words and the important buildings or landmarks. Go over your route again, using the flashcards to focus on the key words. Display these where the children can see them.

Pair the children and ask them to take turns in telling their partners their own routes to school. Encourage them to give sufficient (but only relevant) detail, use the flashcard words and mention **landmarks**. They may need to be aware of other landmarks on their routes – for example, saying 'Turn left at the church opposite the park gates', rather than just 'Turn left at the church'.

When both children in each pair have finished, bring the group together to discuss what they found easy or difficult. Ask one or two children to give their own directions to the group. Pick up on good points and suggest improvements. Return the children to their pairs to try again. Explain that this time you will join them to write their directions down. Each child will end up with four or five written sentences.

With the group, look at the 'A great day out' sheet (photocopiable page 120). Focus on the 'how to get there' map section. Point out that maps or pictures can help to make directions clear. Look at the leaflets and focus on the 'how to get there' sections, reinforcing the key points about using landmarks and **direction words**.

During this lesson or a subsequent lesson, the children could draw basic maps of their routes to school to illustrate their written directions. The maps and writing could be brought together in a book of *Our Routes to School*.

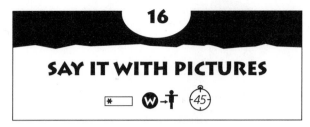

SAY IT WITH PICTURES

Teaching content

Instructions contain important **telling words** or **action words** [imperatives] which the audience needs to know and understand. Pictures can help to make these clearer or to provide hints.

What you need

A chalkboard or sheet of newsprint; photocopiable page 167, writing materials; sheets of card (for display).

What to do

Divide the class into groups and give each a name as below, or use the usual group names. Give each group an instruction in turn, for example:

Blue group	STAND UP.
Yellow group	COME to the gathering area.
Green group	WALK over here and STAND beside me.
Red group	TUCK your chairs in.
Orange group	SIT on the carpet.
All groups	SIT DOWN and LISTEN to me.

Ask the children whether they can recognise the important action words you have used. Can they tell you which words were the action or doing words: which words told or asked them to do something? List these on the chalkboard.

Figure 3

Remind the children that, during lessons, the teacher often tells them what to do. Sometimes you do this by talking, and sometimes you use writing. Ask the children what words you use to tell them to do things. Add these to the list on the chalkboard:

draw	build	glue/stick
write	read	work together
make	paint	stop

You will end up with a very long list of classroom action words. See how many of the children can read all of these words. Doing so will probably prove too difficult for them, which will allow you to introduce picture clues to help the children read the words. Figure 3 shows a possible example.

Tell the children that they are going to design pictures to help each other read the telling words that appear in the classroom, on the wall and on worksheets or cards. Give each child a copy of page 167 and ask them to complete it individually.

When the children have illustrated each action word on the sheet, bring them together to look at the results. Explain that you are going to display some of these in different areas of the room, where they will be relevant. You might enlarge them with the photocopier. Others might be copied and used for worksheet/card instructions, or mounted on card and made into a picture-word matching game. All of these activities will help the children to recognise these important words in written form.

17

WARNING SIGNS

Teaching content

Road signs give instructions. Some of these instructions are warnings, which are given in triangles. The picture and sign shape together convey the message.

What you need

Photocopiable pages 168 and 169, writing and drawing materials (including red pens or pencils).

What to do

Ask the class whether they can think of any warning signs they have seen, such as 'Wet paint', 'Children crossing' or 'Beware of the dog'. Make sure they understand that a warning sign is an instruction telling people to be careful.

Give them copies of page 168*. Can they see anything similar about the warning signs here? Elicit the response that they are all in triangles. Explain that in road traffic signs, all warnings are given in red triangles.

Encourage the children to look at the pictures on page 168 and to think about what they show and what they mean:

- *What does this show?*
- *What do you think it means?*
- *What danger does it warn motorists about?*
- *Why is a sign like this needed?*

Model this with a few other warning signs, making it clear to the children that the picture and the sign shape convey the message. Ask the children to think about the playground or their journey home. Is there anything that they might want to warn other children about? Help them to compile a list of their ideas, such as:

- puddles;
- bullies;
- running without looking;
- broken glass;
- stray dogs;
- crossing the road;
- parked cars;
- strangers.

Give each child a copy of page 169. Ask them to look at the two completed signs. What do these mean?

Tell the children that, working individually, they will now design the next four signs based on some of the ideas listed.

When they have finished their individual pictures, the children should work in pairs to 'read' each other's warning signs. Can they suggest any improvements which would make the warnings clearer?

Take a little time to review the activity with the whole class; then suggest that some children might make large-scale copies of some of their signs for display in an appropriate place. Discuss the choice of place with the children; signs for display out of doors will need plastic covers.

*From *A Highway Code For Young Road Users* (Department of Transport and Local Authority Road Safety Officers Association, 1996).

18

PAINT MIXING

Teaching content
Pictures in a sequence can convey a series of instructions.

What you need
Photocopiable pages 170 and 171 (teacher needs to add colours to page 170 beforehand); an appropriate range of paint colours (including white) in separate tubs; spoons, paintbrushes and empty tubs.

What to do
This activity is best carried out with a group of six children. Explain to the group during choosing time that they are going to work in pairs to follow the pictorial instructions on the 'Paint mixing 1' sheet (photocopiable page 170). You are not going to explain any further, because you want to see whether they can 'read the pictures' and follow the instructions.

Supply them with the appropriate materials and give each pair a copy of page 170 (with the colours filled in where named). Each pair will need three empty tubs, three paintbrushes and one spoon for each original colour. They should use the empty tubs to experiment with paint mixing, recording the results on the sheet.

When the children have completed the activity, bring them together to discuss the results and the process:
• What colours did they make?
• How did they make the grey colour?

• Was it easy to understand the pictures?
• Did they agree throughout?
• Did they become confused at any point?

Discuss with the group how, using photocopiable page 171, they could now design a similar worksheet for another group. Give each pair a copy of page 171. The children should add the colours and/or colour names to the first two pots in each sequence. The completed sheets can be given to another group, as a task; the second group can be asked to evaluate these worksheets.

19

DON'T DO THAT

Teaching content
Pictures can give instructions telling us what **not** to do. Clear instructions can be given by simple signs, using pictures without text.

What you need
Photocopiable pages 172 and 173, writing and drawing materials (including red pens or pencils).

What to do
Gather the class together and give out copies of photocopiable page 173. Ask the children whether they have seen signs like these before. If so, where? Taking each picture in turn, ask the children to say what the sign is telling them **not** to do. Where might they see this sign?

Now ask the children to think about a sign they could make for the classroom. Discuss some of the things they are not allowed to do in the classroom. What might they draw inside the red circle? Suggestions may include:
• Don't shout.
• Don't run.
• Don't drop litter.
• Don't bring your dog.
• Don't go to sleep.

Encourage the children to be creative in their suggestions for instructions and appropriate pictures.

Give out copies of page 172, which provides a template for a DON'T sign. Ask the children to draw their picture first, then colour the border of the circle red, then draw a red line across the circle. Finally ask them to write underneath what the sign says (for example, *Don't chew gum*).

When the sheets have been completed, examine some of the children's pictures. Cover up the writing and ask the others to suggest what instruction the sign is giving, before revealing the words underneath. Use this opportunity to evaluate the clarity of the match of drawing and print in each sign.

At the end of the session, all the children's signs could be collated in a class book with the title *Things You DON'T Do in our Classroom*.

20

AT THE AIRPORT

Teaching content
Signs in everyday places provide information and give instructions and directions.

What you need
Photocopiable page 174, enlarged to A3 size; blank sheets of A4 paper, drawing materials; gummed labels (or small pieces of gummed paper); a chalkboard or large sheet of paper.

What to do
Gather the children together and show them an enlarged copy of page 174, showing an airport scene. Ask them to look at the signs and tell you what instructions they give. Focus on the signs indicating Post Office, Telephones, Restaurant and Departures (top right), and draw the

children's attention to the simplicity of their format: word(s), arrow and picture. Ask the children why the signs need to be kept clear and simple. They may suggest:
• People don't have time to read a long message.
• There isn't enough space to write a lot of words.
• Some people may not be able to read.
• Pictures have the same meaning for people from different cultures.

Now look again at the picture and ask the children to draw upon their own experiences (or imagination) to answer the question: *What other signs might you see at an airport?* They may suggest signs for trolleys, toilets, gate numbers, lifts and so on. List their ideas on a chalkboard or large sheet of paper. Ask the children to suggest other places where such signs might be found – for example, a railway station, a shopping centre, a bus terminus.

Tell the class they will now work in groups of four to make a drawing of an airport, a railway station or a shopping centre. Give the groups time to talk about what will be in their drawings and what signs they might see. Take some feedback about their ideas (to check that they are on the right track), reminding the children that their signs should be simple, concise and easy to identify or read.

Give each group a blank A4 sheet, drawing materials and enough gummed paper labels for what they plan to do. Explain that you want the

group members to work together on this: two will draw the picture and the other two will design the signs, using the gummed labels to stick them onto the finished picture. (The results will vary depending on the children's age and ability.)

Finally, provide time for the groups to exchange their pictures and talk about the signs they have made. Display some pictures in the classroom and discuss them. What signs were included? Are all the signs clear and appropriate?

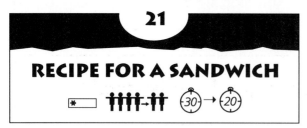

RECIPE FOR A SANDWICH

Teaching content
In a recipe, the sequence of words and pictures gives instructions on how to prepare something to eat.

What you need
Ingredients and equipment for sandwich-making activity (sliced bread, soft butter or spread, four plastic knives, fillings such as lettuce, tomato, cucumber, hard-boiled egg); word cards (see below); photocopiable pages 175 and 176, scissors, glue sticks.

What to do
This activity should be carried out with a group of up to eight children, seated around a table. Each child should have a partner to work with. Supply a tray with the sandwich-making

ingredients (see above) and word cards for the different items. Let the children help you place a word card beside each item: **bread**, **butter**, **knife**, **filling** and so on.

Give each pair a copy of photocopiable page 175, explaining that the recipe needs to be sorted out before they can use it. Give them the recipe frame sheet (photocopiable page 176), which will help them to arrange the recipe. Explain that their first task is to cut up page 175 and place the pictures and words correctly on page 176. Draw their attention to the three headings on the latter sheet:
- Title ('Recipe for a Salad Sandwich').
- What you need.
- What you do.

Also remind the children that they can refer to the word cards on the ingredients tray. Provide each pair with a pair of scissors and a glue stick.

When they have completed their recipe sheets, check that these are correct. If so, the children can progress to making the sandwiches according to the recipe.

Note: It may be helpful to invite a parent to assist the children with the sandwich making. Make sure that there will be enough pieces of sandwich for all the children to have a taste.

Further development
A possible follow-up activity would be to have the groups invent new sandwich fillings or combinations, then use page 176 to write and illustrate their own recipes. These could be gathered together to form a class sandwich recipe book, which could be used by children in other classes or by parents and others.

SAND RULES

Never throw sand at people.

Never throw sand on the floor.

Always brush the floor when you have finished.

Never eat sand.

Only four can play here.

Tidy up the toys after you.

DOMINO RULES

How to play dominoes

Knock if you cannot go.

Share out the dominoes equally.

Take turns, one after the other in order.

Match your domino to one on the ends of the line.

The winner is the first person to have no dominoes left.

1	2	3	4	5

Scholastic
NON-FICTION WRITING
Workshop

MAKING A BIRTHDAY CARD

How to make a birthday card (for_____)

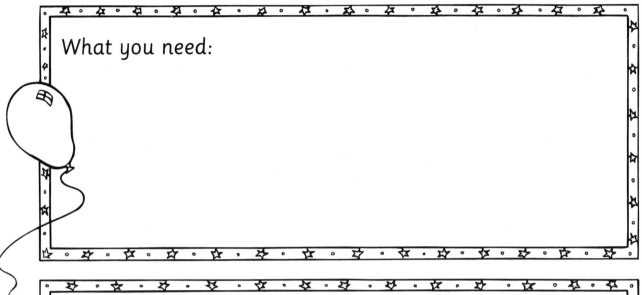

What you need:

What you do:

1.

2.

3.

NAME

TREASURE ISLAND

Help Pirate Pam to find the treasure.

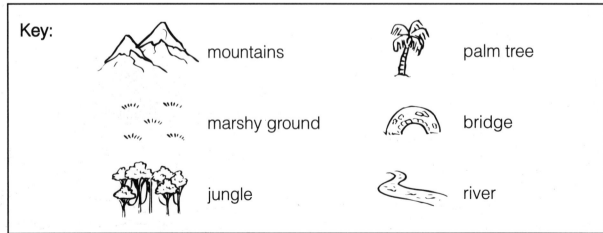

Key:

mountains

palm tree

marshy ground

bridge

jungle

river

Scholastic
NON-FICTION WRITING
Workshop

THE BURIED GOLD

To find the treasure:

1. First walk through the marshy ground.

2. Follow the path signed 'To the beach'.

3. Turn again at the cairn and flag.

4. Follow the path through the mountains.

5. Go across the bridge.

6. You will find the treasure between three palm trees.

Beware of the poisonous spiders.

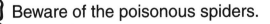

NAME

MIXED-UP INSTRUCTIONS

Recipe for chocolate cake

Put in a tape.

Go up a ladder.

Wait at the big door.

How to get to the assembly hall

Press the red button.

Sift the flour.

Keep moving until
you come to a snake.

How to use the video

Stand up.

Throw a 6 to start.

Spread chocolate all over it.

How to play Snakes and Ladders

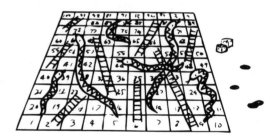

Rewind to the beginning.

Go to the end of the corridor

Put two eggs in a big bowl.

Scholastic
NON-FICTION WRITING
Workshop

DIAL-A-PIZZA

How to order a pizza by phone

1. Phone your order and give your name.

2. Put on the television.

3. Go to collect the pizza and pay for it.

4. Sit on a chair.

5. Take the dog for a walk.

6. Shout 'I love pizza'.

7. Decide what kind of pizza you want.

8. Open the window.

9. Look at the menu.

10. Wave your hands in the air.

FOREST GUIDE

Flowers only	Trees everywhere	Grandma's cottage
No elephants	A winding path	No children allowed
Path closed	This way to Grandma's house	Little Red Riding Hood's House

NAME

FOREST FACTS

Dear Little Red Riding Hood,

Here are the directions from your house to
Grandma's cottage. We hope you get there safely.

Love from

_____

Scholastic
NON-FICTION WRITING
Workshop

INSTRUCTIONS AND DIRECTIONS 155

NAME

SEQUENCE FRAMES

Can you make a tower like mine?

Words to help you: first put then next last

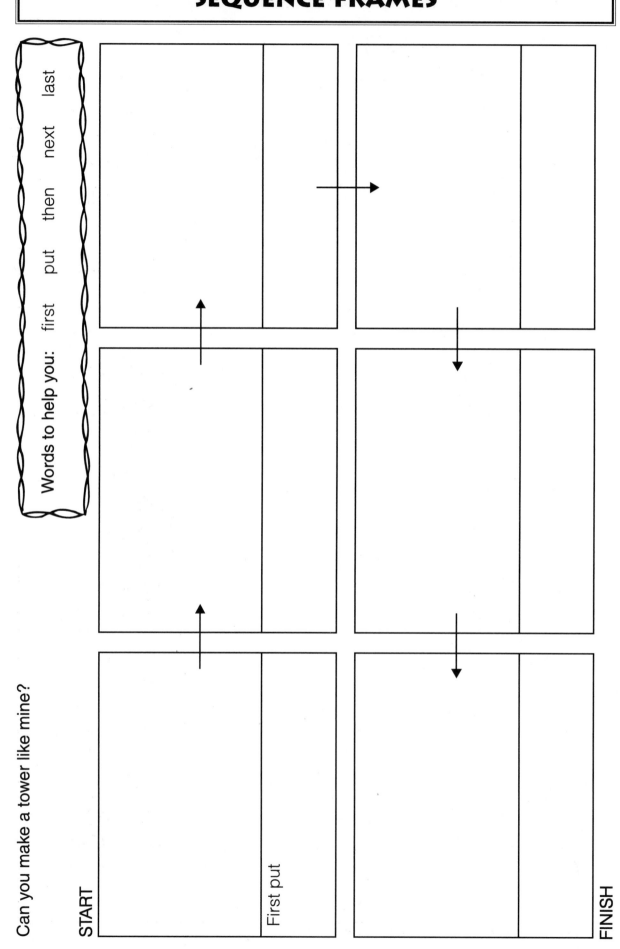

START

First put

FINISH

Scholastic
NON-FICTION WRITING
Workshop

RECIPE FOR BOY SOUP

Recipe for Boy Soup

Ingredients:
(to serve one greedy wolf)

One boy (medium-sized)

One large iron pot

One ton of potatoes

One oodle of onions

One wooden tub of turnips

One cartload of carrots

One packet of fruity chews

One well-full of water

One barrel of bricks

One trowel

Method:

1. *First catch your boy.*
2. *Wash him thoroughly, especially behind the ears.*
3. *Place him firmly in the iron pot.*
4. *Add water, potatoes, onions, turnips, carrots and fruity chews to taste.*
5. *Sit on the barrel of bricks and stir with the trowel until Thursday.*

From *Beware of Boys* by Tony Blundell (Picture Puffin, 1993)

RECIPE FOR GIRL SOUP (1)

Can you organise the recipe to help the wolf make girl soup?

Title:

Ingredients: (to serve one greedy wolf)

Method:

1.

2.

3.

4.

5.

RECIPE FOR GIRL SOUP (2)

Sit on the stones and stir with the spade until Sunday.

one bag of onions

one bag of potatoes

one large iron pot

six sticks of celery

Add water, potatoes, onions, celery, carrots and mints.

Wash her thoroughly, especially the feet.

Place her firmly in the iron pot.

one spade

one girl (large-sized)

one packet of mints

one tin of carrots (large)

one well-full of water

one box of stones (to sit on)

First catch your girl.

TO OPERATE THE PHOTOCOPIER

The photocopier is in the school office.
Please ask the school secretary to let you use it.

To make one copy:

1. Turn on the red switch. 	2. Wait for the green light to show. 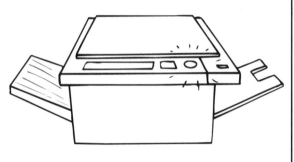
3. Put your master sheet under the flap (face down). 	4. Press the green light. 
5. Take your copy from the tray. 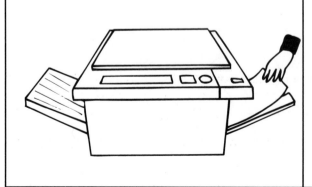	6. Lift up the flap and remove your master sheet. 

Scholastic
NON-FICTION WRITING
Workshop

TO OPERATE THE VIDEO RECORDER

The video recorder is in _____

To record a programme:

1. Turn on

2. Put in

3. Press

When the programme has finished:

4. Press

5. _____

6. _____

To play back a recorded video:

1. _____

2. _____

3. _____

TELLING WORDS

Mum or Dad or Gran tells me to:

I tell my friend to:

*

*

me

my friend

FURRY FRIEND

Choosing Your Cat

In selecting a healthy kitten look for the following:

clean ears

clear, bright eyes

alert, happy nature

damp, moist nose

healthy, pink tongue

sleek, well-groomed coat

strong, firm limbs and feet

licked clean.

a good appetite

From *How To Look After Your Cat* by Colin and Jacqui Hawkins (Walker Books, 1982)

NAME

WHAT TO LOOK FOR

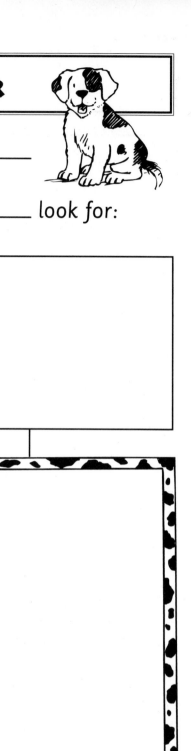

How to choose a _____

When choosing a _____ look for:

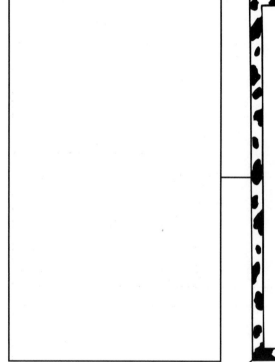

OUR OWN RULES

Rules for

1.

2.

3.

4.

5.

by _____

BREAKFAST

Finally, eat your cereal.

Next, pour milk onto your cereal.

First, pour the cereal into the bowl.

Then sprinkle sugar on top.

SAY IT WITH PICTURES

Draw a picture to match the word:

read	
write	
paint	
build	
draw	

NAME

ROAD SIGNS

INSTRUCTIONS AND DIRECTIONS

Warning signs

These are usually triangular.

Road works

Slippery road

Danger – words describe the danger

Children going to or from school

Steep hill downwards

Crossroads

Roundabout

Uneven road

Cycle route ahead

Road narrows on both sides

Traffic signals ahead

Pedestrian crossing ahead

Two way traffic ahead

Information signs

These are usually rectangular

One way street

Recommended route for pedal cycles to place shown

Route for pedestrians to place shown

Tourist attraction

On approaches to junctions

From *A Highway Code For Young Road Users* (Department of Transport and Local Authority Road Safety Officers Association, 1986)

Scholastic
NON-FICTION WRITING
Workshop

NEW WARNING SIGNS

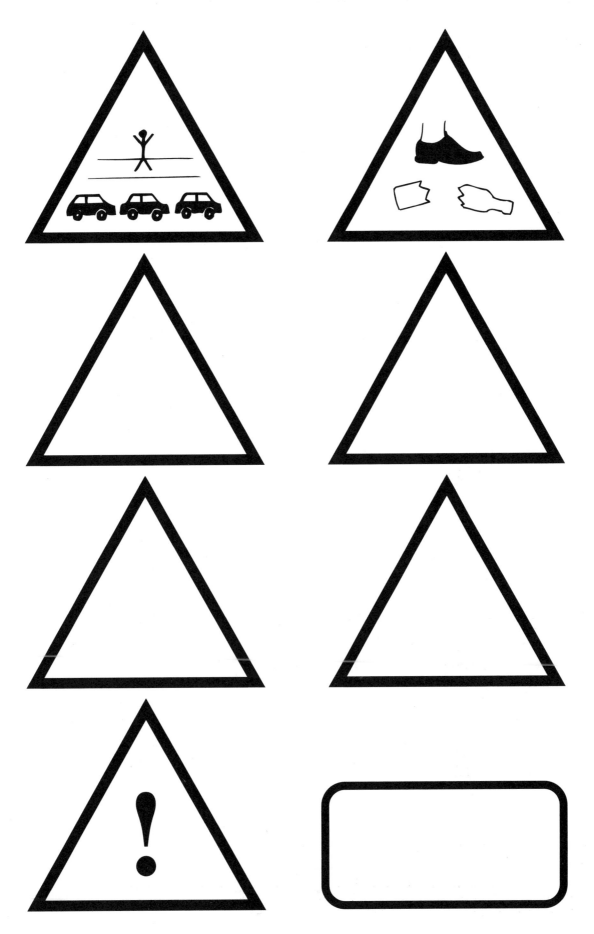

PAINT MIXING (1)

Mix

blue

+

yellow

=

?

red

+

blue

=

?

yellow

+

red

=

?

?

+

?

=

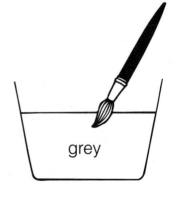
grey

Scholastic
NON-FICTION WRITING
Workshop

PAINT MIXING (2)

Mix

 +  =

 +  =

 +  =

 +  =

DON'T (1)

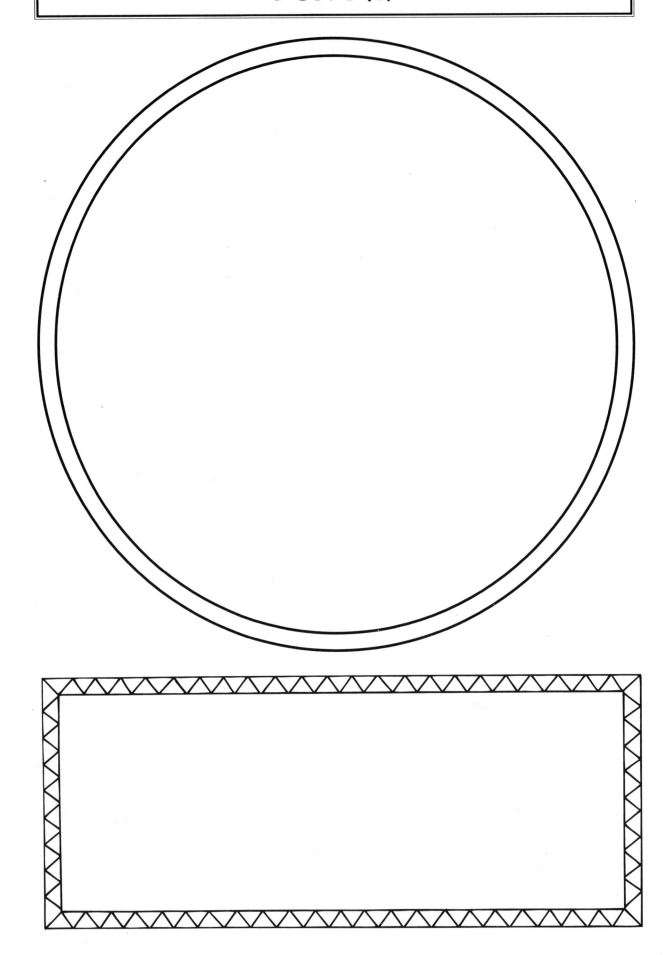

172 INSTRUCTIONS AND DIRECTIONS

Scholastic
NON-FICTION WRITING
Workshop

DON'T (2)

NAME

AT THE AIRPORT

← Post Office
Telephones →
Restaurant →
Departures
Flight To Time Remarks Gate
KP 650 Paris 09.00 Now boarding 12
IG 432 New York 09.00 Now boarding 9
JB 049 Munich 09.15 6
CG 250 Amsterdam 09.45 15
LR 054 Tokyo 09.50 3
SG 350 Rome 09.50 10
Quay Airlines
Departures →
← Arrivals

SANDWICH COURSE (1)

Cut out the pictures and the words to make the recipe for a salad sandwich.

You will need:
scissors and a glue stick.

filling	knife
butter	bread

Put in the filling.

Cut into four pieces.

Close the sandwich.

Butter the bread.

SANDWICH COURSE (2)

Recipe for a Salad Sandwich

What you need

What you do

1.

2.

3.

4.